The Story of English
in 100 Words

Also by David Crystal

The Cambridge Encyclopedia of language

The Cambridge encyclopedia of the English language

The stories of English

The fight for English

Think on my words: an introduction to Shakespeare's language

Txting: the gr8 db8

By hook or by crook: a journey in search of English

A little book of language

Evolving English: one language, many voices.

Begat: the King James Bible and the English language

Internet linguistics

Just a phrase I'm going through: my life in language

The Story of English in 100 Words

David Crystal

ST. MARTIN'S PRESS   NEW YORK

www.stmartins.com

ISBN 978-1-250-00346-1

First published in Great Britain by PROFILE BOOKS LTD

10 9 8 7 6 5 4 3 2

Contents

Preface

How can we tell the story of the English language? There seem to be two main ways. The usual approach is to provide an overview, identifying general themes and trends within the major periods of development: Old English ... Middle English ... Early Modern English ... Modern English. Authors give as many examples of usage within each period as space allows. It's a method I've often used myself, in such books as *The Stories of English*. Its strength, to apply an old metaphor, is that readers obtain a clear view of the wood; its weakness is that they see very few of the trees.

The opposite approach can be seen in the many popular wordbooks that present a series of interesting English words and phrases. One book on my shelves explores the origins of words in personal names, such as *sandwich* and *frisbee*. Another explores the origins of interesting idioms, such as *it's raining cats and dogs*. I've used this method too, such as in my collection of international proverbs, *As They Say in Zanzibar*. Now we have the opposite strength and weakness: readers see lots of trees but do not obtain an overall picture of the wood.

The present book brings together these two perspectives. It is a wordbook, as its chapter headings illustrate, but one with a difference. Every word has been selected because it tells us something about the way the English language developed. And in the course of exploring each one, I move from the particular to the general, relating the word to important themes and trends in the language as a whole. A sense of linguistic history is reinforced by the ordering of the chapters, which is broadly chronological. And the approach has its surprises. Words such as *and* and *what* are not usually included in wordbooks, but they too have a story to tell.

It is, of course, a personal list. If you had to choose 100 words to represent the English language, they would certainly be different. These are mine.

A short history of English words

The Anglo-Saxon monk Bede, writing in his monastery in Northumbria in about the year 730, gives us an early account of those who first spoke the English language. In his *Ecclesiastical History of the English Nation*, written in Latin, he tells us that the island 'contains five nations, the English, Britons, Scots, Picts and Latins, each in its own peculiar dialect cultivating the sublime study of Divine truth'. And he goes on to explain how this situation came about.

The first arrivals, Bede says, were Britons (we would now call them Celts), and they gave their name to the land. The Picts then arrived in the north, from Scythia via northern Ireland. The Scots arrived some time later, and secured their own settlements in the Pictish regions. Then, 'in the year of Rome 798' (= 43 AD), Emperor Claudius sent an expedition which rapidly established a Roman presence in the island.

The Romans ruled in Britain until the early 5th century, when Rome was taken by the Goths and military garrisons were withdrawn. Attacks on the Britons by the Picts and Scots followed. The Britons appealed to Rome for help, but the Romans, preoccupied with their own wars, could do little. The attacks continued, so the Britons came to a decision. As Bede recounts:

> They consulted what was to be done, and where they should seek assistance to prevent or repel the cruel and frequent incursions of the northern nations; and they all agreed with their King Vortigern to call over to their aid, from the parts beyond the sea, the Saxon nation ... Then the nation of the Angles, or Saxons, being invited by the aforesaid king, arrived in Britain with three long ships.

The Anglo-Saxon Chronicle reports their landing in Ebbsfleet (Pegwell Bay, near Ramsgate, Kent) in 449 AD. And within 250 years, it would seem from the earliest records, the language we now know as Old English (sometimes called Anglo-Saxon) achieved its distinctive character.

English vocabulary

Vocabulary is always a primary index of a language's identity, simply because there is so much of it. Anyone who has tried to learn a foreign language knows that the pronunciation and basic grammar can be acquired relatively quickly, but the task of word-learning seems to have no end. Vocabulary is indeed the Everest of language. And it is a mountain that has to be scaled if fluency is to be attained.

In the case of English, the task has been made more complex by the range and diversity of its vocabulary – a reflection of the colourful political and cultural history of the English-speaking peoples over the centuries. To change the metaphor: English is a vacuum-cleaner of a language, whose users suck in words from other languages whenever they encounter them. And because of the way English has travelled the world, courtesy of its soldiers, sailors, traders and civil servants, several hundred languages have contributed to its lexical character. Some 80 per cent of English vocabulary is not Germanic at all.

English is also a playful and innovative language, whose speakers love to use their imaginations in creating new vocabulary, and who are prepared to depart from tradition when coining words. Not all languages are like this. Some are characterised by speakers who try to stick rigidly to a single cultural tradition, resisting loanwords and trying to preserve a perceived notion of purity in their vocabulary (as with French and Icelandic). English speakers, for the most part, are quite the opposite. They delight in bending and breaking the rules when it comes to word creation. Shakespeare was one of the finest word-benders, showing everyone how to be daring in the use of words.

So a wordbook about English is going to display, more than anything else, diversity and individuality. There are few generalisations that apply to the whole of its lexicon. Rather, to see how English vocabulary evolved, we must distinguish the various strands which have given the language its present-day character.

Germanic origins

We begin with the Germanic origins of the language, which can be seen in the early inscriptions that used a form of the runic alphabet widespread in northern Europe. Runes are found on monuments, weapons, ornaments and many other objects, including some very unusual ones (**1 roe**). The Germanic character of English is also visible in the place-names of ancient Britain (**2 lea**), and in the 'little' words that show grammatical relationships (**5 out, 10 what**). By the 7th century, we find the earliest surviving manuscripts in Old English, first in the form of glosses and then in texts of continuous prose, several displaying distinctive scribal abbreviations (**3 and**). However, the actual name of the language is not recorded until the 10th century (**13 English**).

Loanwords

English has never been a purely Germanic language. On the mainland of Europe, the Germanic languages had already incorporated words from Latin, and these arrived in Britain with the Anglo-Saxons. Latin then continued to be an important influence, introducing everyday words to do with plants and animals, food and drink, buildings, household objects and many other domains (**6 street**). This vocabulary continued to expand, with the growing influence of missionary activity reflected in an increase in words to do with religion and learning. Old English also contains a few Celtic words (**12 brock**) – not many, but enough to remind us of the earlier inhabitants of the island.

Scandinavia provided another source of words in the Anglo-Saxon period, but only after a considerable passing of time. The Vikings made their presence felt in Britain in the 780s, attacking the south coast and then the monasteries in the north. Conflict continued for a century, until the Treaty of Wedmore, around the year 880, between King Alfred and the Danish leader Guthrum, established an area of eastern England which, because it was subject to Danish laws, came to be known as the Danelaw. A few Old Norse words are found in Old English writings, but the vast majority are not seen until the 13th century. The earliest Middle English literature shows hundreds of Norse words in use (**20 skirt, 22 take away**).

But the Latin and Norse elements in English are small compared with the huge impact of French in the Middle Ages – a consequence of the dominance of French power in England after 1066 and of French cultural pre-eminence in mainland Europe. Anglo-Saxon words could not cope with the unfamiliar domains of expression introduced by the Normans, such as law, architecture, music and literature. People had no alternative but to develop new varieties of expression, adopting continental models and adapting traditional genres to cope with the French way of doing things. The early Germanic vocabulary, reflecting an Anglo-Saxon way of life (**4 loaf,**

7 mead), gave way to a French view of the world which affected all areas of life, from food (**17 pork**) to law (**18 chattels**), and introducing new forms of address (**19 dame**). The new words usually replaced the old ones, but more often the old words survived, sometimes developing a different meaning (**21 jail**) or stylistic use (**30 royal**).

The international contacts made by British explorers, traders and travellers began as a trickle in the 14th century (**33 taffeta**) and by the 16th century had became a flood (**39 potato**). The renaissance of learning brought a renewal of contact with Latin and Greek, so much so that the number of classical words entering English actually generated huge controversy (**41 ink-horn**). Not all welcomed the change in the language's lexical character. For some, the arrival of classical loanwords made the language elegant; for others, the effect was to make it alien. An argument in favour of keeping the Germanic character of English began in the 16th century and has been with us ever since (**74 speech-craft**). But nothing has ever stemmed the flow of loanwords into the language, and the range was greatly increased by the global spread of English.

American English was the first major variety of the language to emerge outside of the British Isles. It did not take long before the early explorers began to use words from American Indian languages (**45 skunk**), and these along with many others helped to develop an American identity (**58 Americanism**).

From the 17th century on, the geographical hori-
zons of the language steadily expanded as the British
Empire grew and English began to be adapted to
meet the communicative demands of new cultures.
A language soon shows the effect in its vocabulary
of being in a new location, especially when we are
dealing with such dramatically different parts of
the world as India (**48 lakh**) and Africa (**62 trek**).
A regionally distinctive English vocabulary involving thousands of items can emerge within just a few
years. In addition to loanwords, the local culture
will adapt native English words, giving them different forms and meanings (**68 dinkum, 69 mipela**).
The process of borrowing continues today, largely
motivated by economic and cultural factors (**70
schmooze, 78 robot, 96 sudoku**).

New varieties

The earliest records of English were inevitably formal
in character, illustrating a 'high style' of literary
expression, or reflecting such specialised domains as
religion, law and politics. The linguistic creativity of
the Anglo-Saxon age is seen in its riddles (**9 riddle**)
and poetic forms (**11 bone-house**), and illustrates
an imaginative strand of expression that continued
through Middle English (**16 swain, 35 gaggle**) and
Early Modern English, reaching a high point in the
coinages of the Elizabethan era (**43 bodgery, 44
undeaf**). The playfulness is no less important today,
as shown by invented words (**82 doobry, 83 blurb,**

90 bagonise), comic effects (**84 strine**) and the creations of modern fiction (**97 muggle**).

Doubtless Anglo-Saxon society demonstrated the same range of everyday colloquial expression that we have today – human nature hasn't changed so much in a thousand years – but almost all the texts that survive from the Old English period are formal or oratorical in character, and there is hardly any sign of the rhythms and vocabulary of ordinary conversation. Things begin to change in the 11th century. An informal, earthier vocabulary begins to appear in writing, and we see the origins of many modern taboo expressions (**15 arse, 24 cunt, 47 bloody**), as well as words reflecting everyday sounds (**23 cuckoo**), playful coinages (**35 gaggle**) and a wealth of idioms (**31 money**). English society in all its diversity is vividly represented in the writing of Chaucer and the Elizabethan dramatists, notably Shakespeare, and it is not long before enthusiasts start collecting the colloquial words of their age, especially those belonging to the criminal fraternity (**64 dragsman**), illustrating a fascination with slang that has continued to the present day (**66 dude, 86 grand**).

Regional vocabulary has also played its part in the increasing diversity of the language. Dialect variation can be seen from the outset (**8 merry**), and as English came to be established in new geographical locations we see the proliferation of local words and phrases (**26 wee, 42 dialect, 73 y'all**). During the Middle Ages, the need to facilitate communication between all parts of Britain led to the gradual emergence of an increasingly standardised form of written English. Several influential factors were involved, such as the arrival of printing (**29 egg**), the growth of a national civil service, the popularity of major authors (such as Chaucer) and the prestige of biblical translations (**37 matrix, 46 shibboleth**). The formation of a standard English, with an agreed spelling (**32 music**), grammar (**34 information**) and terminology (**38 alphabet**), took several centuries, and at times was highly controversial, especially when people argued the case for spelling reform (**40 debt**). Indeed, the controversies are with us still, as can be seen in words which still have variant spellings (**51 yogurt**), the varying reactions to non-standard spellings (**88 gotcha**) and debates over correctness in grammar (**61 ain't**) and pronunciation (**76 garage**).

Two views of vocabulary

Vocabulary is different from other areas of language, such as grammar and spelling, in that it offers us a direct insight into the social milieu, ways of thinking and cultural innovations of a period of history. Some words inform us about the structure of society (**55 polite, 65 lunch**) or its social practices (**49 fopdoodle, 53 tea, 95 jazz**). We encounter emerging professions (**52 gazette**) and monitor progress in science (**60 species, 75 DNA**) and technology (**63 hello, 99 unfriend, 100 Twittersphere**). We are confronted with new attitudes and mindsets, as we see people looking critically at vocabulary (**81 doublespeak, 89 PC, 93 cherry-picking**). When we explore the history of words, we find a window into society. It is a major theme of this book.

But there is a second way of looking at vocabulary: to examine the techniques the language makes available to build the words that form this history, and this strand also needs to be prominent in a word-book. One important method, as we have already seen, is to borrow the words from other languages. But there are many other techniques of word formation. A Germanic language element can be combined with an element from another language, such as French or Latin (**36 doable**). Words can be reduplicated (**56 dilly-dally**), shortened (**57 rep, 59 edit, 92 app**), conflated (**67 brunch, 98 chillax**), compounded (**91 webzine**) or abbreviated (**79 UFO, 94 LOL**). A suffix can turn into a word (**72 ology**), as can a prefix (**87 mega**). Names can become words – first names (**28 valentine**), surnames (**85 Alzheimer's**), place-names (**80 Watergate**) and product names (**77 escalator**).

But perhaps the most interesting side to vocabulary is when the exploration of word origins (etymology) brings to light results that are unexpected or intriguing. We see people adapting the language in order to make sense of it (**14 bridegroom**). We see extraordinary reversals of meaning over long periods of time (**25 wicked**). We see confusions of meaning (**50 billion**) and disputes over usage (**54**

disinterested). And we see some totally unexpected links between words (**27 grammar**). Not all word origins are known, and there have been some long-standing arguments (**71 OK**). But every etymology at some point takes us by surprise. As I was research-ing each chapter of this book I learned something new about the history of English words – and you will too.

The Story of English
in 100 Words

Roe
the first word (5th century)

In the dry summer of 1929, the crew of an RAF aircraft took photographs of the site of the important Roman town of Venta Icenorum – 'the market-place of the Iceni'. The site is about three miles south of Norwich, in Norfolk, next to the church of Caistor St Edmund. When the pictures were developed, a remarkable street-plan could be seen beneath the fields.

Archaeologists began to excavate the area and discovered a large Anglo-Saxon cremation cemetery on the high ground to the south-east. They found several urns containing remains, and one of them yielded an unexpected linguistic prize. Among a pile of sheep knuckle-bones, probably used as pieces for playing a game, was an ankle-bone (or *astragalus*) from a roe-deer. And on one side of the bone were carved six runic letters.

1. *The runic letters carved into the surface of the roe deer's ankle bone found in the Roman town of Caistor-by-Norwich, Norfolk. The shape of the H rune is especially interesting. It has a single cross-bar, which was characteristic of a northern style of writing. Further south, the H was written with two cross-bars. It suggests that the writer may have come from Scandinavia.*

Turning these into the Latin alphabet, we get the word RAIHAN.

What could it mean? Linguists did a lot of head-scratching. It could be someone's name. An *-n* at the end of a word in the Germanic languages of the time sometimes expressed possession – much as *'s* does in English today. So perhaps the inscription says *Raiha's* or *Raiho's*, telling everyone that this piece belonged to him (or her). But a rather more likely explanation is that it names the animal it comes from: the roe-deer, a species that was widespread in northern Europe at the time.

We can plot the history of the word *roe*. In Old English it appears several times as *raha* or *ra*. And it's seen in some place-names and surnames, such as Rowland ('roe wood') in Derbyshire and Roeburn ('roe stream') in Lancashire. The vowel changed to an *oh* sound in the Middle English period. So *raihan* could mean 'from a roe'.

Why would anyone write such a thing? It was actually quite a common practice. An object, such as a sheath or a pot, would often display the name of its maker or what it was made of: 'Edric made me'. 'Whale's bone,' says the runic inscription on one side of the 8th-century Franks Casket. I can't imagine *raihan* could mean anything other than 'roe', given that it's written on the only bone in the urn to come from a roe-deer. And if it does mean 'roe', then this makes it a candidate for the first discovered word to be written down in the English language.

But is it an English word? The archaeologists

dated the find to the 5th century, and it may even be as early as around 400. That would be well before the arrival of the Anglo-Saxons in 449 – the year we usually think of as marking the start of the Old English period in Britain. The Romans were still in the area then. So maybe the writer was an immigrant who spoke some other language?

There's evidence that at least some of the settlers in Caistor were from Scandinavia. Several of the urns are very similar to those found in Denmark and the nearby islands. So, imagine such a person settling in Norfolk around the year 400. He would have spoken some sort of early Germanic language, such as Old Norse. But it wouldn't have taken him long before he started to speak like the people he met in his new surroundings. Settlers have to adapt quickly, if they want to survive. And if he wrote a word down on an object being used in a game – 'Find the Roe', perhaps? – then surely it would need to be in a form that the other players would understand.

When we do see 'roe' in Old English, a couple of centuries later, it's spelled with *a*, not *ai*. So why did the writer use an *i* in *raihan*? It might represent his original language. Or it might be an old-fashioned way of spelling the word he'd picked up in his new language. Or it might genuinely reflect the way he was pronouncing the word at the time. We'll never know for sure, but my feeling is that the Caistor *astragalus*, now in the Castle Museum in Norwich, is as close as we can get to the origins of English.

Lea

naming places (8th century)

Most people never use the word *lea*. It's a poetic word, meaning a grassy meadow. I remember it especially from Thomas Gray's poem 'Elegy Written in a Country Churchyard':

> *The curfew tolls the knell of parting day,*
> *The lowing herd winds slowly o'er the lea …*

I've never heard it used on its own outside of poetry. And yet we hear it and see it in a hidden form everywhere in daily life.

Lea is one of the commonest elements to turn up in English place-names. It comes from an Old English word *leah* (pronounced 'lay-ah'), meaning an open tract of land, such as a pasture or meadow, natural or man-made. England was heavily forested in Anglo-Saxon times, and it was common practice to make a new settlement by chopping the trees down and starting a farm. If Beorn made a space in this way, it would be called 'Beorn's clearing' – 'Beorn's leah' – modern *Barnsley*.

The word turns up in many spellings. It's commonest as *ley*, but we see it also in such forms as *leigh*, *lee*, *lees*, *lease*, *ly* and *lay*. Sometimes it provides the whole name, as in places called *Lea* or *Leigh*. More usually it is just the way the name ends. But if *lea* is the final element, what does the first element mean?

Often it's the name of someone, as with Beorn.

Someone called Blecca lived in the clearing now covered by modern *Bletchley*. Dudda lived at *Dudley*. Wemba lived at *Wembley*. They are mainly men. Just occasionally we see a woman's name: Aldgyth lived at *Audley*. And sometimes a whole tribe lived in the clearing. *Madingley* means the clearing where Mada's people lived.

The natural features of the clearing often prompted the name. In *Morley* the clearing was moorland; in *Dingley* it was in a dingle. The land must have been level in *Evenley*, rough in *Rowley*, stony in *Stanley* and long-shaped in *Langley*. Also common is a name where the first part describes the trees that used to grow there, as in *Ashley*, *Oakleigh* and *Thornley*. It can be tricky sometimes to work out what the tree-name is. The birch is hidden in *Berkeley*, the bramble in *Bronley*, the yew in *Uley* and the oak in the strange-looking *Acle*.

Some *lea* names refer to what grows in the clearing. It's obvious what this is in the case of *Cloverley*; slightly less obvious in *Farleigh* (ferns) and *Ridley* (reeds). And when the farming started, the name sometimes tells us what was grown (as in *Wheatley* and *Flaxley*) or what animals were around (as in *Durley*, *Gateley*, *Horsley* and *Shipley*, for deer, goats, horses and sheep, respectively). Birds and insects are remembered too, in such names as *Finchley*, *Crawley* (crows) and *Beeleigh*.

Place-names are an integral part of a language, and should always be represented in a wordbook.

Lea is an example of an Anglo-Saxon place-name element. Other such elements are:

> *ham* – 'homestead', as in *Birmingham* and *Nottingham*
> *ing* – 'people of', as in *Reading* and *Worthing*
> *ceaster* – 'Roman town, fort', as in *Chester* and *Lancaster*
> *tun* – 'enclosure, village', as in places ending in *-ton* or *-town*

Each wave of invaders brought its own naming practices. The Vikings settled all over the eastern side of England, establishing hundreds of villages ending in *-by* – the Norse word for 'farmstead' – as in *Derby*, *Rugby* and *Grimsby*. Several French names (such as *Beaulieu* and *Devizes*) arrived in the early Middle Ages.

We always have to be careful, though, when exploring place-names. Often words with different origins have ended up with the same spelling. For example, rivers named *Lea* or *Lee* are hardly going to mean 'forest clearing'. We have to look for the meaning of water names elsewhere. There was a Celtic form *lug-*, meaning 'bright or light', which was also used as the name of a deity. So River Lea may originally have meant 'river dedicated to the god Lugus' or simply 'river which was bright and sparkling'.

And
an early abbreviation (8th century)

Early in the 8th century, monks at the monastery of St Augustine in Canterbury wrote out a long list of English translations of Latin words, in roughly alphabetical order. Towards the end, in the section on words beginning with U, we find the Latin phrase *ultroque citroque* – in modern English we'd say 'hither and thither'. The scribe must have been feeling tired that day, because he glosses it wrongly as *hider ond hider*. The second *h* should have been a *d*. But the phrase is interesting for a different reason: *ond* is an old way of spelling *and*. Doubtless the Anglo-Saxons used the word a lot in their speech, as we do today; but in these ancient glossaries we see it written down for the first time.

Why get so excited over a 'little word' like *and*? In most wordbooks, it's the 'content words' that attract all the attention – the words that have an easily statable meaning, like *elephant* and *caravan* and *roe*. The books tend not to explore the 'grammatical words' – those linking the units of content to make up sentences, such as *in*, *the* and *and*. That's a pity, because these 'little words' have played a crucial role in the development of English. Apart from anything else, they're the most frequently occurring words, so they're in our eyes and ears all the time. In our eyes? The four commonest written words in modern English are *the*, *of*, *and* and *a*. In our ears? The four commonest spoken words are *the, I, you* and *and*. In Old English, *and* is there from the very beginning, and when it appears it's often abbreviated.

We tend to shorten very common words when we write them. *It is* becomes *it's*. *Very good* becomes *v good*. *You* becomes *u* (especially in internet chat and texting). *Postscript* becomes *PS*. The shortened form of *and* is so common that it's even been given its own printed symbol: *&*, the 'ampersand'. The modern symbol is historically a collapsed version of the Latin word *et*: the bottom circle is what's left of the *e*, and the rising tail on the right is what's left of the *t*. The word *ampersand* is a collapsed form too: it was originally *and per se and* – a sort of shorthand for saying '& by itself = and'.

When did people start shortening *and*? We find it in some of the earliest Old English manuscripts. It's written with a symbol that looks a bit like a modern number 7, but with the vertical stroke descending below the line. In some documents, such as wills and chronicles, where strings of words are linked by 'and', we can see 7s all over the page. They're especially noticeable when they appear at the beginning of a sentence.

And at the beginning of a sentence? During the 19th century, some schoolteachers took against the practice of beginning a sentence with a word like *but* or *and*, presumably because they noticed the way young children often overused them in their writing. But instead of gently weaning the children away from overuse, they banned the usage altogether! Generations of children were taught they should 'never' begin a sentence with a conjunction. Some still are.

There was never any authority behind this condemnation. It isn't one of the rules laid down by the first prescriptive grammarians. Indeed, one of those grammarians, Bishop Lowth, uses dozens of examples of sentences beginning with *and*. And in the 20th century, Henry Fowler, in his famous *Dictionary of Modern English Usage*, went so far as to call it a 'superstition'. He was right. There are sentences starting with *And* that date back to Anglo-Saxon times. We'll find them in Chaucer, Shakespeare, the King James Bible, Macaulay and in every major writer. *And God said, Let there be light* … Joining sentences in this way has been part of the grammatical fabric of English from the very beginning. That's one of the lessons the story of *and* teaches us.

Loaf
an unexpected origin (9th century)

Something to eat; something to drink. Words to do with nutrition always play an important part in language history. In particular, the essential role of bread in society, known since prehistoric times, is reflected in a variety of idioms. In English, it can stand for 'food', as in *breadwinner* and the plea for *daily bread* (in the Lord's Prayer). It can mean 'money'. It can identify a state of mind (*knowing on which side one's bread is buttered*) or a level of achievement (*the best thing since sliced bread*).

The surprising thing is that *bread* didn't have its modern meaning in Old English. In one of the word-lists compiled by Anglo-Saxon monks, we find *breadru* translating Latin *frustra* – 'bits, pieces, morsels'. What seems to have happened is that the word came to be applied to 'pieces of bread' and eventually to 'bread' as a substance. It's still used in this way in some dialects: you might still hear someone in Scotland asking for *a piece*, meaning 'a piece of bread'.

So how did the Anglo-Saxons talk about bread? In another list we find a word from the Bible, *manna*, translated by the phrase *heofenlic hlaf* – 'heavenly bread'. We would know *hlaf* today as *loaf*. The *h* stopped being pronounced at the end of the Anglo-Saxon period, and the long 'ah' vowel gradually changed into an 'oh' vowel during the Middle Ages. While that was happening, *hlaf* came to be more restricted in meaning, eventually being used for just the undivided, shaped amount of bread that we now call a *loaf*.

There are very few instances of the word *bread* in Old English, but *hlaf* appears frequently – and in some interesting combinations. The head of a household was seen as the person who provides bread for all, a *hlaf-weard*, literally a 'bread-warden'. A servant or dependant was someone who ate his bread: a *hlaf-æta*, 'bread-eater'. A steward was a *hlaf-brytta*, a 'bread-distributor'. A lady was originally a *hlæfdige*, 'bread-kneader'. That *-dige* ending is related to the modern word *dough*.

Hlaf turned up quite a lot in Christian religious settings too. *Lammas* was 1st August, the day when the eucharistic bread was first baked from the new harvest. That name comes from *hlaf-mæsse*, 'loaf-mass'. Walking to the altar to receive the host was a *hlaf-gang*, a 'bread-going'. Bethlehem, where Jesus Christ was born, was a *hlaf-hus*, a 'house of bread'.

Hlaf-weard changed its form in the 14th century. People stopped pronouncing the *f*, and the two parts of the word blended into one, so that the word would have sounded something like 'lahrd'. Eventually this developed into *laird* (in Scotland) and *lord*. It's rather nice to think that the 'high status' meanings of *lord* in modern English – master, prince, sovereign, judge – all have their origins in humble bread. And it's the unexpectedness of this etymology that qualifies *loaf* to take its place in this book.

Loaf then went on new linguistic journeys. Different kinds of loaves appeared, such as *white loaf* and *brown loaf*. Several derived forms were coined, such as *loaflets* and *mini-loafs* (small loaves), *loaf-shaped* and *loaf-tin*. The shape generated a range of non-bread uses, such as *meat loaf* and *sugar-loaf*. There were technical senses too, such as the religious use of *holy loaf* (for bread distributed at Mass).

But nobody could have predicted the 20th-century

use of *loaf* in Cockney rhyming slang. In fact, two rhymes evolved, but only one survived. The popular usage had *loaf of bread* replacing *head*. It soon reduced to simply *loaf*, especially in the phrase *Use your loaf*, meaning 'use your common sense'. The *Oxford English Dictionary* has references to this expression from 1938, and it seems to have been widely used in forces slang. It has a somewhat dated feel about it today.

The defunct usage had *loaf of bread* replacing *dead*. You can find it in Auden and Isherwood's play *The Dog beneath the Skin* (III.iii.123):

> *Oh how I cried when Alice died*
> *The day we were to have wed!*
> *We never had our Roasted Duck*
> *And now she's a Loaf of Bread.*

Out

changing grammar (9th century)

An easy way of making new vocabulary is to take a word and change it into another word by using it in a different way in a sentence. We take a verb and turn it into a noun. Or turn an adjective into a verb. Any part of speech can have its grammar shifted in this way. The process is technically described as *conversion* or *functional shift*.

English-speakers have been doing this with words

since Anglo-Saxon times. Take a little word like *out*. It could be a verb: to *out* was to 'expel' or 'dismiss'. Or an adverb, as in to *draw out* a sword. Or an exclamation: *Out!* meant 'Alas!', now heard only in some regional dialects. It could be a preposition, as in *out the door* – a usage disallowed in standard English today, though common regionally. An adjective use appears in *the out edge*, where today we'd say *the outer edge*. And from the 17th century it's been used as a noun, as in *the ins and outs* ('the complexities') and *looking for an out* ('a means of avoiding'), as well as in such games as baseball (*two outs*).

New uses continue to emerge. The adjective got a fresh lease of life in the 1960s, when people talked about the *out crowd* ('unfashionable set'). A new verb use followed: to *out* oneself or someone else was to make public an undeclared sexual identity. From there it was a short step to any kind of exposure of private information. Since the 1990s, people can be *outed* as the originator of an idea, a member of an organisation or the parent of a child.

Out is one of thousands of words which have changed their grammar. Such verbs as *laugh, look, push* and *lift* have all become nouns. Adjectives have become verbs (*to calm, to empty*) and nouns (*a nasty, a given*). Nouns have become verbs (*to host, to contact*) and adjectives (*garden chair, railway station*).

Shakespeare was the conversion expert. 'I *eared* her language.' 'He *words* me.' Some of his conversions seem really daring. Even the name of a person can become a verb. 'Petruchio is Kated.' But all he was doing was tapping into a natural everyday usage that is still with us. How many parents haven't said something like this?

> Child (at bedtime): But I want to watch Mickey Mouse.
> Parent: I'll Mickey Mouse you if you don't get those pyjamas on right now!

Even though changes like this are ancient and frequent, people do sometimes dislike conversions. The verb *spend* is known from the 12th century, and developed a new lease of life in the 20th, when businessmen started talking about *advertising spends* and the like. Letters began to appear in the press objecting to this 'horrible new' word.

In fact the usage wasn't new at all. John Bunyan used *spend* as a noun in the 17th century. And the same pedigree is found in noun-to-verb shifts, which are also sometimes criticised. *Author* has been especially disliked: *She's authored a new book.* The first recorded use of *author* as a verb is 1596, but for some reason it continues to attract criticism.

Today, nouns can become verbs in next to no time. Google was launched in September 1998 (*see* §77). People were *googling* by the end of the year.

6 *Street*
a Latin loan (9th century)

The Romans spoke Latin. So, later, did the missionaries that arrived in Britain. As a result, quite a few words of Latin origin came into English in its early years. *Street*, from Latin *strata*, was one of the first. We find it in the earliest Old English manuscripts, written as *stræt* – the *æ* letter representing a long vowel sound a bit like the *a* in modern English *dare*.

When the Anglo-Saxons arrived in Britain, they found that the Romans had already built a network of long, straight, paved roads to supplement the many paths which dated from prehistoric times. They used the Germanic word *weg* ('way') to describe these ancient tracks, which had emerged over time through repeated usage, as in *hrycgweg* ('ridgeway'). They used the Latin word to describe the Roman innovations – *streets*.

The names of the four major Roman highways reflect this difference. *Watling Street* (from London to near Shrewsbury) and *Ermine Street* (from London to the Humber) were Roman roads. *Icknield Way* (from Gloucestershire to south Yorkshire) was prehistoric. What we now call the *Fosse Way* – a Roman road running between Leicester and Axminster – seems to go against this distinction, until we realise that it was originally known as *Fosse Street*. The name *Fosse Way* dates only from the 15th century.

Over 500 words came into English from Latin

during the earliest period of Old English. We can never be sure exactly when they arrived. Some would have been picked up by the Celtic-speaking Britons during the Roman occupation and become familiar to the first Germanic settlers. Some would have been brought over from the continent of Europe in the Anglo-Saxon boats. And the Latin-speaking monks would certainly have added to the number.

The new words expressed a wide range of notions. There were words for plants and animals, food and drink, household objects, coins, clothing, settlements and building materials, as well as to do with military, legal, medical and commercial matters. *Candle* and *kettle*, *cup* and *kitchen*, *cat* and *dragon*, are all originally Latin words. So are *butter*, *cheese*, *sack*, *wall*, *mile* and *wine*.

Words from Latin continued to come into English throughout the Anglo-Saxon period, but they changed their character. The teaching of the Church had to be communicated to the people, so new vocabulary was needed to express the new concepts, personnel and organisational procedures. Words such as *altar*, *creed*, *deacon*, *school* and *philosopher* arrived. So did *grammar*.

Meanwhile, *street* was developing its own meanings and uses. We find several old idioms, such as *by sty and by street* or *by street and stile*. If something happened 'by sty and by street', it was happening 'everywhere'. Another medieval idiom was *to wend one's street*, meaning 'to go one's own way'. And if

2. Terry Pratchett (left), and a character from his Discworld saga, at one of the streets in Wincanton, Somerset, named after a location in the series. Why Wincanton? It had twinned with the fictional city of Ankh-Morpork in 2002.

you *took the street*, it meant you were setting out on a journey. These all died out in the 1500s.

But new uses were arriving. In the 16th century *the street* came to be used for the money-market area of London. In the 18th century we find it referring to a locale for prostitution (*on the street*) as well as a description of the average person (*the man on the street*). In the 19th century, *on the street* developed the meaning of 'homeless'. And the word continued to grow. *Streetwise* arrived in the 1940s. *To be street* – in tune with urban subculture – in the 1970s. It was followed by *street credibility*, soon shortened to *street cred*. In the 1990s *street* became a term for a type of skateboarding.

So what happened to the original meaning of *street*? For a long time it was used as part of a description of the highway, as in *Broad Street* and *Mill Street*. Even today British English keeps the definite article in front of some of these names: we say *I was shopping in the High Street*, not ... *in High Street*. Eventually other criteria were used, such as the name of an important person (*Wellington Street*) or occupation (*Brewer Street*). American English went in for numerals and letters: *M Street, 32nd Street*. Today, virtually any word in the language can be used along with *street*. In 2009 a new road in Wincanton, Somerset, was named after a location in a Terry Pratchett *Discworld* novel: *Peach Pie Street*.

7   *Mead*

a window into history (9th century)

Today we think of mead as a rather exotic alcoholic drink, made by fermenting a mixture of honey and water. In early history it was the alcoholic beverage of choice throughout ancient Europe, Asia and Africa. Some think it was the first fermented drink. It makes frequent appearances in the Germanic folktales of the first millennium and repeatedly appears in Anglo-Saxon manuscripts, such as the epic poem *Beowulf*.

Mead was more than just a drink. It was a symbol of power. If you had the time and luxury to sit around drinking mead, then all must have been well in your land. And conversely: if you didn't have that opportunity, things must have been going badly. At the very beginning of *Beowulf* we are told that the king, Scyld Scefing, 'from bands of enemies, from many tribes, took away mead-benches'. That settles it. They would have been victories indeed!

So it's not surprising to find that there was a large vocabulary of *mead*-words in Old English. Through this single word we obtain a considerable insight into Anglo-Saxon culture and society. A settlement might actually be called a *medu-burh* – a place renowned for its mead-drinkers. Any warrior living there would make nightly visits to the *medu-heall* ('mead-hall') or *medu-seld* ('mead-house') – the equivalent of the modern city hall – where his leader would be holding court and feasting. How would he get there? By walking along a *medu-stig* ('path to the mead-hall') through the *medu-wang* ('land surrounding the mead-hall'). All roads, it seemed, led to mead.

Once inside the hall, the vocabulary of mead was all around him. The place to sit was called a *medu-benc* ('mead-bench') or *medu-setl* ('mead-seat'). He and his fellow-warriors would engage in a lengthy bout of *medu-drinc* ('mead-drinking'), taking a *medu-scenc* ('draught of mead') from a *medu-full* ('mead-cup'). He would soon get *medu-gal* ('enthused by the mead') and experience *medu-dream* ('mead-joy'). If he had too much, he would end up *medu-werig* ('mead-weary').

It's fascinating to see a word being used in this way, permeating so many aspects of social behaviour. And it's a feature of English which we continue to exploit today. *Whisky drinkers* might buy a *whisky bottle* from a *whisky shop* or (in olden days) a *whisky house,* and pour a *whisky peg* from a *whisky decanter* into a *whisky glass.* They might become *whisky sodden* or develop a *whisky voice.* On the other hand, we don't extend the usage as much as the Anglo-Saxons did. We don't usually talk about *whisky seats, whisky paths* or *whisky joy.*

In the Middle Ages, mead changed its social standing in Britain. Wine became the drink of choice among the upper class, leaving mead, along with ale and cider, as the drink of the poor. Mead never died out as a drink, but it took second place to ale and cider, which were much easier to brew. *Ale* is used fifteen times in Shakespeare; *mead* not once.

Gradually, mead came back into fashion, sometimes developing new uses and shifting its meaning. In the 17th century it could be used to mean any sweet drink. Robert Burton used the term *mead-inn* in 1632, referring particularly to Russian drinking practices – a tavern where mead was the main drink sold. People in Britain in the 18th century drank *mead wine*.

In the USA, the name took on a different sense, referring to various sweet carbonated drinks sometimes flavoured with sarsaparilla. Americans continue to be strongly interested in mead today. There's an International Mead Association, and a festival is held every year in Colorado. New *mead*-words continue to be coined. The occasion is a *meadfest*, and many *meaderies* and *mead-lovers* attend. There are *meadmaking* courses, *meadings* (tasting parties) and if you want you can read a *meadzine*.

But beware: don't mix up the 'drink' sense of the word *mead* with another sense which is recorded in English from a few centuries later – a shortened form of *meadow*. When you see such words as *meadflower*, *meadsweet* and *meadwort*, these are all meadow flowers. They have nothing to do with the drink. And if you know a road called the *Meadway*, that's the 'meadow' sense too, and a later development. It's *mead* in the 'drink' sense that fascinates linguists, because it's part of a window into the origins of English.

Merry

a dialect survivor (9th century)

The first time we see the word *merry* is in an Old English manuscript, made by or for King Alfred, at the end of the ninth century. Except we don't actually see *merry*, spelled like that. What we see is *myrige*, which would have been pronounced something like 'mi-ree-yuh'.

There were many words in Old English written with that letter *y*. It seems to have represented a vowel sound pronounced high up in the front of the mouth, a bit like the *i* of *sit*, but with rounded lips. We can hear the same sound today in the way many Scots people pronounce *you*, or the way the French say *tu*. By the Middle Ages, people must have stopped rounding their lips, because the scribes started writing the word with an *i*. Middle English manuscripts show such spellings as *miri* and *mirye*.

In Anglo-Saxon manuscripts we also see the word spelled as *muri* and *meri*. That suggests there were different dialect pronunciations in the country. And when we look at where the people who wrote the manuscripts were located, we can indeed begin to see a dialect pattern. The scribes who used the *i* spelling were based in the south, around Winchester. Those who used *u* came from further west. And those who used *e* came from the south-east, in Kent.

By the Middle Ages, there was a huge tangle of spellings. Over fifty ways of spelling *merry* have been recorded. Versions with *e*, *u* and *i* turn up all over the place. And then, gradually, the spelling with *e* won, reflecting the pronunciation which had become the norm in London and the south-east.

What could be *merry*, in Old English? The word originally meant 'something that causes pleasure', so it was used for all kinds of things and happenings. Songs, birds, harps, organs and voices could all be merry. So could the weather, the countryside, days, winds and smells. Books and stories were merry. So were clothes and jewellery. And the sun and stars. And countries. *Merry England* dates from around 1400.

Only in the 14th century did the word come to be applied to people, and then it developed a remarkable range of uses. Merry England indeed! We see it used for any kind of animated enjoyment – and also when the animation is drink-fuelled. Anyone happily tipsy is said to be merry. That usage goes back to the Middle Ages, when people were also said to be *merry-drunk*. In the 16th century, strong ale was called *merry-go-down*.

One sign of a word becoming really established is when it turns up in idioms, book titles, nicknames and compound words, and from the 14th century we see it in a whole host of phrases. Idioms? *Make merry* and *the more the merrier*. Titles? *The Merry Wives of Windsor* and *The Merry Widow*. Nicknames? *The Merry Monarch* (Charles II) and the *Merry Men* (of Robin Hood). Compounds? The supremely descriptive

merry-totter and *merrythought*. A merry-totter was a
medieval name for a children's swing or see-saw.
It's still heard today in some regional dialects, especially in Yorkshire. And in the 16th century, a merrythought was a word for a fowl's wishbone, pulled
and broken while each party made a wish.

The process continued in later centuries. In the
18th century we find the arrival of the fairground
carousel – a *merry-go-round*. In the 19th century we
find people being *merry and bright* and *going on their
merry way*. *Merry-go-up* was a slang name for snuff.
The Royal Navy came to be called the *Merry Andrew*.
In the 20th century, we find *merry maids* used as the
name of a wide range of enterprises, from milk choc-
olate caramels to domestic cleaning services. And in
the USA and the Caribbean, *merry* became popular
as a verb. One could *merry oneself* ('amuse oneself').
And people could *merry up*, such as after a drink, or
merry up a room if it looked dull.

The ultimate accolade was when *merry* came to be
used, in the 16th century, as a greeting for one of the
chief festivities of the year. *Merry Christmas!* And, for
a while, *Merry New Year* too, until *Happy* took over.
Not a bad career for what was originally a Kentish
dialect word.

Riddle

playing with language (10th century)

People have probably played with words as long as language has existed. They love to take a word and mess about with it, such as by saying it backwards, making an outrageous pun on it or stringing it together with other words so that it can't be said (tongue-twisters). The playful temperament has produced innumerable word games and competitions, such as crossword puzzles and Scrabble. And one of the earliest signs of this temperament in English appears in the form of riddles.

It took a while for the word *riddle* to develop this meaning. When it first appears in Old English, in early translations from Latin, it was in the form *rædels* (pronounced 'reah-dels'), a combination of the word for 'read' with an *-els* ending. It meant a 'reading' or 'opinion' about something. Gradually the sense broadened to an 'interpretation' of something, and then, in an interesting switch, to a 'saying that defies easy interpretation' – an enigma. The modern meaning was in place by the 10th century.

The form of the word changed too. That *-els* ending was quite common in Old English, turning up in such words as *gyrdels* ('girdle') and *byrels* ('tomb' – think *buriels*). But during the 14th century it evidently confused everyone. By then, the *-s* ending on a noun was being thought of as a plural. So when people saw the word *redels* (as it was usually spelled in the Middle Ages), they thought of it as a plural form, *riddles*. During the 15th century, they gradually dropped the *-s* to make a new singular form, *riddle*.

There's a collection of Old English riddles in one of the finest Anglo-Saxon manuscripts: the Exeter Book. It was compiled in the late 10th century, and is so called because it was acquired by Bishop Leofric for Exeter Cathedral some time afterwards. It contains over thirty poems and over ninety verse riddles. They cover a wide range of subjects reflecting the Anglo-Saxon way of life, such as weapons, book-making, animals and everyday objects.

Each riddle presents a topic in a mysterious or puzzling way and asks the reader to identify it. Some are the equivalent of the modern 'dirty joke'. The riddle whose answer is 'a key' begins like this: 'Something wondrous hangs by a man's thigh ...' Here's R. K. Gordon's translation of one of the cleaner riddles:

> I saw a creature in the cities of men who feeds the cattle. It has many teeth. Its beak is useful. It goes pointing downward. It plunders gently and returns home. It searches through the slopes, seeks herbs. Always it finds those which are not firm. It leaves the fair ones fixed by their roots, quietly standing in their station, gleaming brightly, blowing and growing.

The answer is: a rake.

The story of *riddle* doesn't end here. By the 14th century it had developed the general sense of a 'difficult problem' or 'mystery'. It came to be applied to people: *He's a complete riddle; I don't understand him at all!* And then, in the 16th century, the noun became a verb, meaning 'to speak in riddles'. 'Lysander riddles very prettily,' says Hermia in Shakespeare's *A Midsummer Night's Dream* (II.ii.59).

Something very curious then took place. Some people started to use the verb and the noun together. *Riddle me a riddle*, says one 16th-century writer, meaning 'Solve this riddle for me'. Others dropped the noun and used the verb twice: *Riddle me, riddle me.* Evidently people found the sound of the word appealing. And children did too, because eventually the phrase became part of a popular nursery rhyme:

> *Riddle me, riddle me, ree;*
> *A little man in a tree;*
> *A stick in his hand,*
> *A stone in his throat,*
> *If you tell me this riddle*
> *I'll give you a groat.*

Riddle-me-ree became a frequent title for collections of riddles, and the phrase often appeared in children's stories. You'll find it in *The Tale of Squirrel Nutkin*, by Beatrix Potter.

What
an early exclamation (10th century)

Imagine the scene. You are in front of an audience, about to make an announcement or give a speech. Everyone is noisy. Some may have had too much to drink. You need to quieten people down. You've no hammer to bang against a table. There's no spoon to clink against a glass. All you have is your voice. At least you can shout. But what will you say? 'Ladies and gentlemen ...'? 'Quiet, please ...'? 'Excuse me ...'? They all seem a little weak.

The poet-minstrels in Anglo-Saxon mead-halls had the same problem. They were called *scops* (pronounced 'shops'), and their role was to tell the heroic stories of the Germanic people to the assembled warriors. The scops must have had prodigious memories. The epic poem *Beowulf* is 3,182 lines long – that's about the same length as Shakespeare's *Romeo and Juliet* – and, if it was recited in one go, without interruptions, it would have taken a scop well over three hours. But first he had to call the assembly to order. And he did this with a single word, which appears as the opening word of that poem: *Hwæt!* It is one of the first oral exclamations in English to achieve a literary presence. Nine Old English poems begin with the word.

How was *hwæt* pronounced? The letter *æ* was like the short *a* of modern English *cat* as spoken by someone from the north of England. The *h* shows that the *w* was pronounced with aspiration – a puff of air. Anyone today who makes a distinction in their speech between *whales* and *Wales* is using the old *hw* sound. And if we turn the whole word into modern spelling, it appears as *What!*

Hwæt certainly packs an auditory punch. Scholars usually translate it as 'Lo!', or as a story-telling opener such as 'Well now' or 'So', but nothing quite captures the short sharp impact of a *Hwæt!* With its open vowel and high-pitched final consonant, it's a vocal clap of the hands. We can easily imagine a hall of warriors falling silent, after such an attention-call.

What! continued to have an exclamatory use throughout the Middle Ages, when the word came to be spelled in the modern way and gradually broadened its meaning. It began to express surprise or shock. It could be used to hail or greet someone, in the manner of a modern *Hello!* And it acted as a summons. In *The Tempest* (IV.i.33), Prospero uses it to call his spirit-servant to him: 'What, Ariel! My industrious servant, Ariel!'

We don't use *what* as a greeting or summons any more. The closest we get to that is in the phrase *What ho!*, which lasted well into the 20th century in Britain, and is still sometimes heard. Its fashionable use among the upper classes led to a neat parody by P. G. Wodehouse in *My Man Jeeves* (1919):

> 'What ho!', I said. 'What ho!' said Motty. 'What ho! What ho!' 'What ho! What ho! What ho!' After that it seemed rather difficult to go on with the conversation.

What! is still used today as an exclamation of surprise or astonishment, often tinged with irritation or anger. We can expand it with an intensifying phrase: *What the devil! What the dickens! What on earth!* And if our emotion is so great that we're at a real loss for words, we simply leave the sentence hanging in the air: *What in the name of ...! What the ...!*

What, spelled *wot*, was especially visible as an exclamation in the mid-20th century, during and after the Second World War, when everything was in short supply. All over Europe appeared the drawing of a man with a small round head, a long nose and two hands, peering over the top of a wall. He was called Mr Chad, and he was always complaining about shortages, using such phrases as 'Wot, no eggs?' or 'Wot, no petrol?' In the USA he was called Kilroy, and a similar cartoon contained the caption 'Kilroy was here'. In Australia, 'Foo was here'.

The origin of *Chad* is uncertain, but it's likely to derive from the nickname of the cartoonist George Edward Chatterton, who was known to everyone as *Chat*. The caption became a catch-phrase, and it stayed popular long after wartime shortages disappeared. It's still with us. In recent months I've seen the drawing on a wall where someone was complaining about the lack of a good mobile phone connection. The writing said simply: 'Wot, no signal?'

3. The name may vary, but the face remains the same – one of the most widely travelled pieces of 20th-century graffiti. Theories abound as to the origins of the names Chad, Foo and Kilroy, with several real-life candidates suggested. The character has been given other names too. In the British army, for example, he was called 'Private Snoops'.

Bone-house
a word-painting (10th century)

What comes into your mind when you hear the word *bone-house*? It sounds like a building where someone has put a number of bones – animal bones, perhaps. Or maybe human. I once visited an ancient monastery church in Belgium, and in the crypt, on shelf after shelf, were the skulls of innumerable generations of monks. That felt like a bone-house. But whichever way you look at it, bone-houses are for the dead. Charnel-houses, we would call them these days – from the Latin word for 'flesh', *carnis*. Flesh-houses.

The Anglo-Saxons used the word. *Ban-hus* (pronounced 'bahn-hoos') it was then. But they used it to talk about something very different: the human body while still alive. It paints a wonderful picture. That's what we all are, at the end of the day. Bone-houses.

Evidently the picture was an appealing one, for the poets coined several words for the same idea. They also describe the body as a 'bone-hall' (*bansele*, pronounced 'bahn-selluh'), a 'bone-vessel' (*ban-fæt*, 'bahn-fat'), a 'bone-dwelling' (*ban-cofa*, 'bahn-cohvuh') and a 'bone-enclosure' (*ban-loca*, 'bahn-lockuh'). The human mind, or spirit, was a *ban-huses weard* – 'guardian, or ward, of the bone-house'.

This sort of vivid description is found throughout Anglo-Saxon poetry. It's one of the earliest signs of an impulse to create figures of speech in English literature. It was an impulse that extended well beyond English, for similar word creations appear in the early poetry of other Germanic languages, such as the Viking tongue, Old Norse. But the Anglo-Saxon poets really took it to heart. There are over a thousand such descriptions in the great Old English saga *Beowulf*.

The coinages are called *kennings*, a word adapted from the Old Icelandic language. *Kenning* is from the verb *kenna*, 'to know', and it captures the idea that these coinages have a meaning that is more insightful than can be expressed by a single word. *Ken* is still used as a verb in Scots English and in some northern dialects of England. And we still hear it as a noun in the phrase *beyond our ken*.

The poets loved kennings, because they were opportunities to vary their descriptions when they told long stories of heroes and battles. Stories of this kind repeatedly refer to the same kinds of events, such as a battle, or a banquet or an army crossing the sea. We can easily imagine how a story could get boring if the storyteller said 'And he crossed the sea in a boat' a third, fourth or tenth time. How much more appealing would be fresh, vivid descriptions – especially ones that would suit the rhythm of the verse and echo the sounds of other words in his lines.

So, what could a ship be? A *wave floater, sea goer, sea-house* or *sea steed*. And the sea? A *seal bath, fish home, swan road* or *whale way*. Anything could be described using a kenning. A woman is a *peace-weaver*, a traveller is an *earth-walker*, a sword is a *wolf of wounds*, the sun is a *sky candle*, the sky is the *curtain of the gods*, blood is *battle sweat* or *battle icicle*. There are hundreds more.

Kennings don't seem to have been much used outside of poetry, and they fell out of use after the Anglo-Saxon period. But the same poetic impulse lies behind many compound words. We hear it still when a scientist is described as an *egghead*, or a criminal as a *lawbreaker* or a boxer as a *prize-fighter*. But we don't seem to take the same joy in creating vivid alternative descriptions as the Anglo-Saxons did.

Perhaps we should. Imagine a football sports commentary, for example, in which the commentators used kennings. They'd be talking about *net-aimers* and *ball-strikers* and perhaps, when things got exciting, *score-cuddles*, *card-offs* and *ref-haters*. Am I misremembering, or have I sometimes heard the occasional off-the-cuff kenning in a commentary? If so, without realising it, the bone-house is tapping into a tradition that is a thousand years old.

Brock
a Celtic arrival (10th century)

During the 11th century, several books were written which listed the names of plants and animals, especially in relation to their medicinal properties. In one of the first, around the year 1000, we read this:

'Sum fyðerfete nyten is, ðæt we nemnaþ taxonem, ðæt ys broc on Englisc.' Translation: 'There is a four-footed animal, which we call taxonem, that is brock in English.'

Brock, the Old English name for a badger. It was the everyday name until the 16th century, when *badger* took over in standard English. Why the change? Probably because *brock* had developed a number of unpleasant associations: people would talk about a *stinking brock*, and by 1600 the word had come to be applied to people who were dirty or who behaved in an underhand way – much as someone might use the word *skunk* today. In Shakespeare's *Twelfth Night* (II.v.102), Sir Toby Belch sees Malvolio puzzling over the meaning of a letter and says *Marry, hang thee, brock!* Malvolio is indeed, badger-like, rooting out the sense. But Toby is also calling him a stinker.

Badger, by contrast, had positive associations in the 16th century. The word probably comes from *badge*, the white mark on the animal's head being its most striking feature. Badges had strongly positive associations, being chiefly associated with the 'badges of arms' used by knights. The word was also being used, in the sense of a 'distinguishing sign', in the 16th-century translations of the Bible. So if people wanted an unemotional way of talking about the animal, *badger* would be more appealing.

But *brock* didn't disappear. It stayed as the everyday name for the animal in regional dialects all over the British Isles and was especially popular in the north of England. Then it started to creep back into standard English – as a name. *Brock the badger*. It has appeared in countless sympathetic accounts of badgers by naturalists, and is the regular name used in children's stories, most famously by Alison Uttley. Few other dialect words have achieved quite the same press.

Brock feels so English – so it comes as a bit of a surprise to discover that it isn't Anglo-Saxon at all. It's Celtic. We find it in Irish, Scottish Gaelic and Manx as *broc*, in Welsh and Cornish as *broch*, in Breton as *broc'h*. The animal goes under a quite different name in the Germanic languages, such as *grævling* in Danish and *Dachs* in German (dachsunds were bred to be badger hounds). It didn't come over with the Anglo-Saxons. That's what makes it linguistically interesting. It's one of the very few words to have come into Old English from the Celtic language spoken by the ancient Britons.

Hardly any Old English words have a clear Celtic connection. There are a large number of place-names in England of definite Celtic origin, such as *Avon*, *Exe* and *Severn*, and all the names beginning with *pen* ('hill'), such as *Penzance* and *Penrith*. But if we restrict the search to everyday words, in addition to *brock*, we find *crag*, *wan*, *dun* ('grey-brown'), *bannock* ('piece of a loaf or cake') and a dozen or so others. A few more might have had a Celtic origin, such as *puck* ('malicious spirit') and *crock* ('pot'), but similar-looking words appear in the Scandinavian languages, so we can't be sure.

Why did the Anglo-Saxons ignore the Celtic words they would have heard all around them? There are many conflicting explanations. Perhaps the two ways of life were so similar that the Anglo-Saxons already had all the words they needed. Or perhaps there was so little in common between the Celtic way of life as it had developed in Roman Britain and the Anglo-Saxon way of life as it had developed on the continent that there was no motivation to borrow Celtic words. There might even have been a conscious avoidance of them. If the Celts were forced out of England by the invaders, as some people believe, then one of the consequences would be a distaste for all things Celtic, especially the language. On the other hand, some Anglo-Saxon noblemen gave their children British names, such as Cerdic and Cedd. Cædwalla, for instance, was king of Wessex in 685, according to the Anglo-Saxon Chronicle, and his is a distinctly Welsh name.

Whatever the reasons, Celtic words are conspicuous by their absence in Old English. *Brock, crag* and the others remain as an intriguing reminder of what might have been.

English
the language named (10th century)

Much of what we know about the early history of Britain comes from *The Ecclesiastical History of the*

English Nation, written in Latin around 730 by the Northumbrian monk Bede. He tells us how, in the 5th century, 'three of the most powerful nations of Germany – Saxons, Angles and Jutes', arrived in the British Isles. It isn't possible to say exactly where they came from, or even whether they were as nationally distinct from each other as Bede suggests. But one thing is clear: two of those nations gave us the name *Anglo-Saxon*.

It's first found in 8th-century Latin writers, who used the phrase *Angli Saxones* to mean the 'English Saxons' (of Britain) as opposed to the 'Old Saxons' (of the continent). The *Angli* part was the impor-tant bit, in their mind. It was the crucial, contrastive element – the *English* Saxons, as opposed to other kinds. Only later did the phrase come to mean the combined Germanic people of Britain.

In the 9th century, the name broadened its meaning. In the Treaty of Wedmore, made between King Alfred and the Danish leader Guthrum around the year 880, we see *English* opposed to *Danish*, and it plainly refers to all of the non-Danish population, not just the Angles. Also, at around the same time, *English* is used for the language. When Bede's book was translated into Old English, we find several passages which take a Latin name, and then say '… this place is called in English …', giving the English equivalent.

English came first; *England* came later. It took over a century before we find the phrase *Engla lande*

4. *This scribe at work is probably Bede. The picture is in a 12th-century book from the north-east of England,* The Life and Miracles of St Cuthburt.

referring to the whole country. There was then a long period of varied usage, and we find such forms as *Engle land*, *Englene londe*, *Engle lond*, *Engelond* and *Ingland*. The spelling *England* emerged in the 14th century, and soon after became established as the norm.

Some strange things happened to *English* as the centuries passed. As the language spread to other countries, such as the USA, Australia and South Africa, people started talking about American English, Australian English and so on. This meant that, whenever anyone wanted to talk about the language as it was used in England (as opposed to Britain), they had to use the curious repeated form: *English English*. And since the early 20th century the word has had a plural, *Englishes*, referring to the kind of English used in a particular region of the world. People talk of the *new Englishes* developing in such countries as Singapore and Nigeria – dialects of English, but on a grand scale.

Anything associated with England attracted the adjective. In the 15th and 16th centuries, an often fatal sweating sickness (probably a type of influenza) was called the *English sweat*. In the 18th century, foreigners would describe people who were feeling especially low or depressed as having the *English malady* or *melancholy*. At roughly the same time, we see the emergence of the *English breakfast* – a substantial meal consisting of hot cooked food, such as bacon, eggs, sausages and suchlike. It was the contrast with the rest of Europe which was being noted: they just had *continental breakfasts*. And a similar contrast appeared during the 19th century: an *English Sunday*, with everything closed, was contrasted with a *continental Sunday*. In the USA, an interesting use developed in billiards and pool when a player hits a ball on one side so that it spins, affecting the way it bounces off another ball. It must have been an originally British technique, because the idiom is *put English on the ball*.

People never seemed quite sure how to handle the word *English*. In the 17th century, translating something into the language was said to *Englify* or *Anglify* it. In the early 18th century it was *Anglicised* – a usage that evidently didn't please everyone, for later in the century we find both *Englishified* and *Englishised*. Today it seems to have settled down as *Anglicise*, but there's still some variation in usage.

Anglo- and its derivatives have come to dominate, but there's still some room in the language for *Saxon*. Celtic speakers sometimes refer to English people as *Saxons* and their language as *Saxon*, and the word is hidden within the Scots Gaelic (usually) jocular term *Sassenach*. Words in English that are of Germanic origin (as opposed to those from Latin and the Romance languages) are often called *Saxon* words. So there's some life in the old word yet.

Bridegroom

a popular etymology (11th century)

What has a man about to be married got to do with someone who looks after horses? People have come up with some crazy explanations. Perhaps, in a male-dominated society, the man was thought to be 'grooming' his bride, or giving her the value of a horse? Or perhaps, more romantically, he was going to carry her off on his horse? The truth is less exciting, but linguistically more illuminating.

The word for a man about to be married, or just married, is first found in an Anglo-Saxon version of the Gospel of St John, but it turns up in an unfamiliar form: *brydguma*. This is a compound of *bride* and *guma*, which was a somewhat poetic Old English word for 'man'. Half a millennium later, in William Tyndale's translation of the same Gospel, it appears as *brydegrome*. Why the change?

During the Middle English period, the word *guma* fell out of use. Probably most people never used it at all, for the recorded instances are all very literary. It must have been an odd experience, hearing the word *brideguma* when someone got married. Everyone knew what *bride* meant, but *guma* was a mystery.

And so people, unconsciously, turned it into something more familiar. The change seems to have taken over a century. The latest example of *brideguma* – spelled *bredgome* – recorded in the *Oxford English*

Dictionary is 1340; the earliest example of *bridegroom* – spelled *brydegrome* – is 1526.

Why did people replace *gome* with *groom*? Because the sound and the meaning of the two words were very close. When *groom* first arrived in English, in the 13th century, it meant simply 'man-child', 'boy'. It then broadened its meaning to apply to adults, and soon seems to have been restricted to a particular kind of adult male – someone who had an inferior position in a household. By the 16th century, this sense of 'servant' had narrowed further to mean an attendant who looks after horses, and this is the primary sense today – though the older use is still seen in the titles of some members of the British royal household, such as *Groom of the Chamber*.

So, at the end of the Middle English period, when *guma* was disappearing, *groom*, meaning 'man', would have been a natural replacement. And thus we have the modern form, which basically means nothing more than 'bride's man'.

The history of English has many examples of this kind of development – what is called 'popular' or 'folk' etymology. When people encounter an unfamiliar word, they often try to make sense of it by relating it to a word they already know. And if enough people make the same guess, the new formation can become part of the language. We see popular etymology operating again when we *button-hole* people: we've quite forgotten that originally what we were doing was 'button-holding' them. And it's there when we jocularly call *asparagus* 'sparrow-grass'.

Arse
an impolite word (11th century)

Arse wasn't an impolite word when it first arrived in English. It simply meant an animal's rump, and we see it recorded in writing, from around the year 1000, in all kinds of straight-faced settings, such as glossaries, poems and scholarly works. A 14th-century writer tells us solemnly that 'haemorrhoids are fine veins that stretch out at the arse'. And in the 16th century the word even turns up as part of a sermon: 'How arseward [i.e., perverse] a thing it is for every man to be given to his own profit,' says the preacher. No hint of vulgarity here.

But things didn't stay that way. It was inevitable that, as soon as the word began to be used for the human posterior, the association with animals and with excrement would turn it into a 'dirty word'. We can sense this when we see people searching for a more polite expression. We find *bum* and *buttock* in the 14th century, the latter soon shortened to *butt*, which later became popular in the USA. *Backside* appeared in the 16th century and *posterior* soon after. The high regard for politeness in 18th-century society led to several alternatives – *bottom* and *behind*, as well as the scientific *gluteus maximus* and the fastidious *derrière*. In the USA, the 19th century introduced a genteel pronunciation, *ass*. And as the politer terms increased, so did the rudeness level of *arse*.

An early development was the application of

the word to a whole person. *Heavy arse*, meaning a lazy fellow, is recorded in the 1500s. In Britain and Ireland it became a slang name for a fool – a usage which proved very popular in the 20th century, when comments such as *I made a right arse of myself* were increasingly heard. The verb also became widespread: to *arse about/around* is a ruder version of *fool about/around*.

The last century also saw the word becoming popular in the British Isles as an exclamation. On its own (*Arse!*), it's used as an expression of annoyance, a little stronger than *Damn!* and very much stronger than *Oh no!* In the form *my arse!* it's a scornful rejection of opinion – a ruder version of *Nonsense!* and more focused, as it's usually attached to words that the other person has said. 'You seem a bit nervous,' says A. 'Nervous my arse!' ripostes B. That's quite a strong comment. Anyone wanting to retain the force but avoid the rudeness could substitute *My foot!*

Arse is one of the 'taboo words' of English, whose role is so important in everyday speech that, despite the controversy they arouse, they need to be well represented in any word-list. But it's important to appreciate that attitudes to taboo words vary greatly over time and place. There are huge differences of opinion over just how rude a word like *arse* is.

Several expressions have retained their force, such as when a person is described as being pretentious (*He's up his own arse*) or is given a contemptuous rejection (*Kiss my ass!*, *Up your ass!*), and compounds such as *arse-licking* and *arsehole* are widely accepted as pretty rude. On the other hand, intensifying expressions such as *boring the arse off someone* (being extremely boring) or *working my arse off* (working extremely hard) are less so. The younger you are, of course, the less these usages will make you turn the slightest hair.

Many people find the force of *arse* reduced when used in phrases, and may not consider such 20th-century expressions as *arse-over-tip* ('head over heels') or *arse about face* ('back to front') as being rude at all. The same applies to some of its uses as a verb, such as *I arsed up my essay*. And the word almost loses its identity in *arsie-versie* or *arsy-varsy* ('upside down', 'back-side foremost'), which was popular in the 1500s and still heard today. It was a jocular adaptaton of *vice versa* (*versa* being pronounced 'varsa' in the 16th century).

Part of the uncertainty is that usage varies around the English-speaking world. The replacement of *arse* by *ass* in American English, universally encountered through US films and television programmes, has resulted in both forms becoming used in British English. A Brit who would never say *arse* in polite conversation might well use the intensifying *I was working my ass off* or talk about someone as being a *smart-ass*. And the unusual expression *ass-backward(s)*, meaning 'completely wrong, back-to-front', has achieved a wider presence too, especially after Thomas Pynchon played around with it in *Gravity's Rainbow* (1974). What's unusual about it, as one of his characters says, is that the ass already faces backwards, so if the expression means 'wrong way round' it should really be *ass-forwards*. But what seems to be happening here is the development of a new, intensifying usage, meaning 'very', heard also in some other slang phrases, such as *ass o'clock* (as in *I gotta get up at ass o'clock tomorrow*, i.e. 'very very early').

We have to be especially careful when it comes to the adjective *arsy*. In Britain, the word means 'bad-tempered' or 'arrogant', as in *We get the occasional arsy customer in here*. In Australia, the word has developed a positive meaning, 'lucky': *That was an arsy goal*. It's wise to pay special attention to who's speaking before deciding what to make of *You're an arsy bastard!*

 ## Swain
a poetic expression (12th century)

It's strange how some words end up only in poetry. Sometimes the reason is to do with the need to keep a particular rhythm in a line – so, if you're looking for a word with a single beat, you can turn *over* into *o'er*, *ever* into *e'er* and *often* into *oft*. But with such words as *lea* (§2), *dewy*, *dusky* and *darksome*, which would be highly unlikely to be heard in everyday speech, it's not at all clear why poets fell in love with them. The story of *swain*, meaning 'lover' or 'sweetheart', is one of the strangest, for there's nothing in its origins to suggest that one day it would become a poet's word. On the contrary. In Old English, a *swan* (pronounced 'swahn') looked after pigs (*swine*).

The word began its journey towards a more refined life in the early Middle Ages. Any young man who held a low social position could be called a *swain* – but, as today, some low positions were higher than others. In particular, the word was used for one of the servants of a knight – the lowest level, below a squire and a groom, but still a desirable career for a young lad. Gradually, *swain* came to be applied to any man who was an attendant or follower, and then it broadened in meaning. When Chaucer describes Sir Thopas as a *doughty swayn*, he means simply 'valiant man', and when in one of the York Mystery plays Jesus is described as a *litill swayne*, the writer means only 'little boy'.

But then another association developed, with shepherds and farm labourers, and this is the one that appealed greatly to poets. In Spenser's *Fairy Queen* (Book III, Canto VI, Stanza 15) we can see the romantic countryside associations beginning to build up: 'the gentle shepherd swains, which sat / Keeping their fleecy flocks'. By the end of the 16th century, a *swain* had become a country wooer. There was even a short-lived derived form, *swainling*, which was sometimes also used for women.

Poetic diction is an important element in the history of vocabulary, but it isn't as popular now as it once was. Today the language of the streets provides most of the lexicon of poetry. We won't find many modern poets using such words as *swain*. But Modern English does retain a couple of echoes of the early 'dogsbody' meaning of the word, in an unexpected place – the world of boats. The original pronunciation has been lost, but the old word is there in the spelling of *boatswain* and *coxswain*.

Pork
an elegant word (13th century)

Why does *foie gras* sound so much more palatable than *goose liver*, or *boeuf bourguignon* more romantic than *beef stew*? The tradition of preferring French words to English ones in menus has a history which dates from the Middle Ages. The Anglo-Saxons would have eaten *sheep, pig, cow* and *calf*; but these words were evidently too crude to satisfy the fastidious manners of the newly arrived French court.

During the early Middle English period, a new set of words became established as the gourmet's norm. People now ate *mutton, pork, beef* and *veal*. The recipe books of the period are full of French words. Here is the beginning of one of them – a 14th-century recipe for fig tartlets. The French words are underlined:

> Tourteletes in fryture. Take figus & grynde hem smal; do þerin saffron & powdur fort. Close hem in foyles of dowe, & frye hem in oyle.

Tartlets in fritter (batter). Take figs and grind
them small; put therein saffron and strong powder
(spice). Wrap them in foils (layers) of dough and
fry them in oil.

You wouldn't get far in the kitchen without French.
The only cookery words that are Old English are
grind and *dough*.

Although *pork* started out within the language
of elegant cuisine, its subsequent history was less
salubrious. Already in the Middle English period the
adjective *porkish* was being used as a rude description of fat ('piglike') people. An obese or greedy
person might be called a *porkling*. *Porky* came later, in
the 18th century, for anything or anyone resembling
a pig, and it became the normal insult for someone
noticeably overweight. Warner Bros reclaimed the
phrase somewhat when the stuttering cartoon character Porky Pig was introduced in the *Looney Tunes*
series in the 1930s. But the general trend was in the
opposite direction. *Pork* continued to pick up negative associations.

In the 20th century, the process continued when
Cockney rhyming slang made *pork pie* a substitute
for *lie*. *Porky pie* was used in the same way, and by
the 1980s this had been shortened to *porky*. 'Don't
tell such porkies,' someone might say. It is a euphemism, humorously softening the force of *lie*.

But the ultimate fall from grace came when *pork*
began to be used for the penis in American slang of
the 1930s. How did that change come about? The

origin seems to lie in the 17th century. The implements used by pig slaughtermen were colloquially called *pigstickers*, and this term soon became slang for any kind of sharp implement, especially when used as a weapon. The association with pigs led to *porker* becoming a slang term for a sword. And the obvious parallels in shape and language (such as *sword thrusts*) led to both *pork* and *pork sword* being used for the male appendage. The French courtiers would have been horrified.

 ## *Chattels*
a legal word (13th century)

It must have been quite hard, being a lawyer in the Middle Ages in England. Originally, all your law books would have been in Latin. Then, in the 13th century, they start being written in French. Then along comes English. Lawyers had a problem. When they wanted to talk about a legal issue, which words should they use? Should they describe the issue using an English word or opt for the equivalent word in French or Latin? And would the words be equivalent anyway? There might be subtle differences of meaning between an English word and a French one which could make all the difference in a court of law.

How to choose? If someone decided to leave all his property and possessions to a relative, should the legal document talk about his *goods*, using the Old English word, or his *chattels*, using the Old French word? The lawyers thought up an ingenious solution. They would use both. If the document said *goods and chattels*, they would be covered against all eventualities. So that's what they did. And the phrase *goods and chattels* is still used in legal English.

A large number of legal doublets were created in this way, and some of them became so widely known that they entered everyday English. Every time we say *fit and proper* or *wrack and ruin* we are recalling a legal mix of English and French. *Peace and quiet* combines French and Latin. *Will and testament* combines English and Latin.

The pattern caught on. After a while, lawyers began to bring together pairs of words from the *same* language. To avoid a dispute over whether *cease* meant the same as *desist* (both words are from French), they simply said that someone should *cease and desist*. That's also why we talk about a situation being *null and void* or someone being *aided and abetted*. English words were combined too – hence *have and hold*, *each and every* and *let or hindrance*. Lawyers sometimes went in for even longer sequences, such as *give, devise and bequeath*. This is one of the reasons legal English seems so wordy. (Another is that lawyers were often paid by the word.)

Chattels has some interesting linguistic relatives. The French word is a development from Latin *capitalis*, and this has given us the word *capital*. It has, less obviously, given us *cattle*. Today we think of cattle as cows, bulls, calves and other bovine animals. But until the 16th century it had a much more general sense. Any group of live animals held as property, or farmed for food or produce, could be called *cattle*. So we find the word being used for horses, sheep, goats, pigs, fowls ('feathered cattle') and even camels. 'Take heed,' says a writer in 1589, 'thine own cattle sting thee not.' He was talking about bees.

Dame

a form of address (13th century)

People are very sensitive about how others address them. The reason is that there are several choices, and each choice carries a nuance. We could guess a great deal about the relationship between the parties if we heard:

> Hello, Mrs Jones
> Hello, Jane
> Hello, Janey
> Hello, Mrs J
> Hello, chick
> Hello, Didi

Very few people know that Jane was called Didi by her family when she was little.

Our preference for using – or not using – titles can alter over quite short periods of time. Young people these days are much readier to use first names on initial acquaintance than are their seniors, and don't so often get irritated when a cold-caller greets them over the phone with a breezy intimacy. It's hardly surprising, then, to find that the use of titles has changed over the course of centuries. But few have had such a chequered history as *Dame*.

Today, the use of *Dame* is very restricted. It's the female equivalent of a knight of an order of chivalry, in the British honours system, and people notice it when someone well known receives it, such as Dame Judi Dench. It also has a limited use elsewhere. Lady baronets and some retired female judges can be called *Dame*. These are the last vestiges of a title which was originally widespread in English society.

When *dame* arrived from French in the 13th century, it was immediately used for ladies of high rank, and for any woman in charge of a community, such as an abbess or prioress. But it quickly went downmarket. By the 16th century, any woman married to a person with social standing, even if relatively low in rank (such as a squire or a yeoman), could be called *Dame*.

At the same time, the word was being used in a general way to describe 'the lady of the house' – a housewife. From there it was a short step to find it used for any mother, whatever her social position. And in the 14th century, a *mother tongue* was often referred to as a *dame's tongue*.

The original vowel in *dame*, coming from French,

was pronounced more like the one we hear in modern English *dam*, and this spelling, along with *damme*, was soon used. But *dam*, perceived to be a different word, began to attract negative connotations. It was used for female animals as well, and when used for a human mother it usually had a tone of ridicule or contempt. The emergence of the phrase the *devil and his dam* didn't help.

In the early 20th century *dame* went further downmarket, especially in the United States, where it became the usual slang word for a woman. 'There is nothin' like a dame' went the refrain (in *South Pacific*). Then a most curious development took place in Britain. In pantomimes it came to be used for a comic middle-aged female character, traditionally played by a man. And the comic overtones spilled over into other comic roles, as in the famous case of Dame Edna Everage (aka Barry Humphries). This is as far away from the upper strata of society as it's possible to imagine.

The higher up the social scale we go, the more strictly the address rules are imposed. At the highest levels, whole books have been devoted to how we should address a prince, a duke, a baroness, a president, a professor, a cardinal, a judge, a mayor ... It can get very complicated, especially in Britain. Is a duke called *Your Grace* or *My Lord*? What about an earl, a marquess or a baron? Most people would have to look up the answer. (All are *My Lord*, except the duke.) Is the sovereign's son called *Your Royal*

Highness? Yes. What about the sovereign's son's son? Yes. And the sovereign's son's son's son? No. Getting it wrong would be a terrible *faux pas*, in some circles.

Skirt

a word doublet (13th century)

When two cultures come together, the words of their languages compete for survival. We can see the process taking place early on in the history of English, following the Danish invasions of Britain. The Danes spoke a language known as Old Norse, and this had many words that had a related form in Old English. What would people end up saying? Would the Danish settlers adopt the Old English words? Or would the Anglo-Saxons adopt the Old Norse ones?

In the event, people went in both directions. During the Middle English period we find Norse *egg* and *sister* ousting Old English *ey* and *sweoster*. And Old English *path* and *swell* ousted *reike* and *bolnen*. But there was a third solution: the Old English and Old Norse words both survived, because people gave them different meanings. This is what happened to *skirt* and *shirt*.

Shirt is found occasionally in late Old English (spelled *scyrte*), with the meaning of a short garment worn by both men and women. *Skirt*, from Old Norse, is known from the 1300s, and seems to have been used chiefly for the female garment – the lower part of a dress or gown. But the word could also be used for the lower part of a man's robe or coat too. And it is this notion of 'lower part of something' which led to the later sense of *skirt* meaning an edge or boundary – hence such words as *outskirts* and *skirting board*.

Shirt and *skirt* went different ways during the Middle English period. *Shirt* became increasingly used only for the male garment, and *skirt* for the female. But the distinction has never been complete. Today, women's fashion includes shirts, and skirts are normal wear for men in many countries (though, kilts aside, rarely encountered in Western culture). Clothing such as the *T-shirt* is gender-neutral. And most of the idioms using *shirt* are too. Both men and women can *bet their shirt*, give away *the shirt off their back* and *keep their shirt on*.

Cases like *shirt/skirt*, where both words survive, are known as *doublets*, and there are many of them in English. From the Danish period, we find Old Norse *dike* alongside Old English *ditch*, and similarly *hale* and *whole*, *scrub* and *shrub*, *sick* and *ill* and many more. There are even more in regional dialects, where the Old English word has become the standard form and the Old Norse word remains local, as in *church* vs *kirk*, *yard* vs *garth*, *write* vs *scrive* and – of especial interest because of its widespread dialect use – *no* vs *nay*.

Jail

competing words (13th century)

One of the most noticeable features of English vocabulary is the large number of words that entered the language as borrowings from French, especially in the period after the Norman invasion of 1066. Some of them are illustrated by the cooking and legal terms that form part of the story of *pork* and *chattels* (§§**17**, **18**). The vast majority of French loans were borrowed just once – which is what one would expect. But on a few occasions, a word got borrowed twice.

Why borrow a word twice? If English speakers were already using it, what would be the point? The answer lies in the fact that the people who introduced these words had different social and linguistic backgrounds. In the early part of the period, they were usually speakers of the dialect of French spoken in Normandy; in the later part, they were people who had learned the French of Paris – the 'posh' dialect that was becoming the standard. Several words had different forms in these two dialects. The Norman version was borrowed first; a Parisian version came along later. And English sometimes kept both of them.

That's why we have both *gaol* and *jail*. The g-spellings are recorded first, in the 13th century: we read about a *gayhol* and a *gayll*. The j-spellings, such as *iaiole* and *iayll* come long later (*i* and *j* weren't

5. In Monopoly, one goes directly to jail, not gaol. Over a hundred local variants of the game have now been licensed. A spin-off dice-game was called 'Don't Go To Jail'.

distinguished as separate letters in the Middle English period). It must have been quite confusing. Which form should one use? Even as late as the 17th century, people were scratching their heads. The point was noted by the political author Roger L'Estrange, writing in 1668: he talks about the 'rage' some people feel because they can't decide 'whether they shall say [write] Jayl or Gaol'.

But at least the meaning stayed the same in this instance. In many other cases of 'double borrowing', the two words developed different meanings. Today, *convey* (from Norman French) doesn't have the same meaning as *convoy* (from Parisian French). Nor are Norman *reward*, *warden*, *warrant* and *wile* the same as Parisian *regard*, *guardian*, *guarantee* and *guile*.

Three hundred and fifty years on, the problem of *gaol* and *jail* is still there in British English. The Americans sorted it out in the 18th century, opting for *jail*, and that's the only form found in the USA today. But Britain kept both. Official legal documents preferred the *gaol* spelling. British and Irish prisons were originally spelled *Gaol*. Oscar Wilde wrote a 'Ballad of Reading Gaol'. In speech, of course, there's no difference: both words are pronounced 'jail'.

Gaol seems to be disappearing from everyday writing nowadays in Britain, though lawyers still use it. And it's still popular in some other countries, such as Australia. Overall it's definitely the junior partner: a mere 2 million hits on Google in 2010, compared with 52 million for *jail*. It's difficult to say just when the replacement trend started. Some people put it down to the influence of the popular board game Monopoly, invented in the USA. When the game was 'translated' into Britain in the 1930s, the non-London squares weren't changed. That's why there is a distinctly American-looking police-man on the 'Go To Jail' square. And suddenly British players were being sent 'directly to jail'.

 ## Take away
a phrasal verb (13th century)

It must have come as quite a shock to Samuel Johnson, slowly working his way through the alpha-bet for his *Dictionary of the English Language* in the early 1750s, when he reached the letter T. The end of his great project was in sight, and then he encoun-tered the verb *take*, with its remarkable number of senses. He had had to deal with complicated verbs before: *come* had ended up with 56 senses, *go* had 68 and *put* had 80. But *take* was going to require an unprecedented 124.

The high total was caused by a large number of combined forms, where *take* was used along with another word, such as *in*, *off*, *up* and *out*, or two words, as seen in *take up with*. These are called *phrasal verbs* in modern grammatical parlance. The combi-nation of words expresses new senses. *Take off*, for example, has such meanings as 'become airborne', 'be successful' and 'remove'. Aircraft and projects can take off. Clothes can be taken off.

Phrasal verbs became an important feature of English vocabulary during the Middle Ages. *Take away* is first recorded around 1300 in its general sense of 'remove' or 'withdraw', and it soon developed special applications. If someone was *taken away*, it could mean he died or was killed. If servants were *taking away*, they were clearing the table after a meal. If something *took away* from an achievement, it detracted from it. And other senses have arrived in modern times. Since the 1930s, we have had the option of eating food in the place where it has been prepared or *taking it away* to eat elsewhere.

A few phrasal verbs take on a second life as nouns. If I *hand something out*, what I deliver is a *handout*. If I tell someone to *go ahead*, I give them a *go-ahead*. And this has happened to *take away* too. In Britain, the shop that sells food that can be eaten off the premises is called a *takeaway* (often hyphenated, as *take-away*), usually with a characterising adjective: a *Chinese takeaway*, an *Indian takeaway*. The word can be used as an adjective too: *a takeaway curry, takeaway hamburgers*. And since the 1970s it has been applied to the meal itself: *We're having a takeaway tonight.* But *takeaway* isn't universal in the English-speaking world. In Malaysian and Singaporean English, they use a Chinese word – *tapau*, food. And American English has opted for different phrasal verbs – *take-outs* or *carryouts*.

Cuckoo
a sound-symbolic word (13th century)

Most words don't resemble the things they refer to. There's nothing about the shape of the word *table* that shows us an object with four legs and a flat surface. And there's nothing in the sound of the word *commotion* that makes us hear a violent disturbance. But English has quite a few words where the opposite is the case: *cough, knock, murmur, zoom, crunch, bang, clatter, teeny, babble, splash, plop* ... The sound of the word seems to imitate the reality to which it refers. Such words are often called *onomatopoeic* – a term from Greek meaning 'word creation' – especially when people are talking about the effects heard in poetry. Linguists call them instances of *sound symbolism*.

Cuckoo is an excellent example of a sound-symbolic word. In many languages the name of this bird echoes the sound of its call. The effect can't be heard so well in the Old English word for a cuckoo, *geac*; but in the Middle Ages it comes across clearly in the form *cuccu*. The earliest recorded use, from the mid-13th century, is in the famous 'Cuckoo Song', the earliest known singing 'round' in English:

> Sumer is icumen in, Lhude sing cuccu

The translation is 'Spring has come in. Loudly sing, cuckoo!' In Middle English, there was no separate word for springtime; *spring* as the name of a season isn't recorded until the 16th century. The word *summer* was used for the entire period between the vernal and autumnal equinoxes.

But even sound-symbolic words can change their meaning and lose their original echoic associations. This has happened to *cuckoo*. In the 16th century we see it being applied to people. The bird has a monotonous call and lays its eggs in the nests of other birds, so anyone engaged in unimaginative repetitious behaviour or doing something perceived to be stupid came to be labelled *a cuckoo*. When Aristophanes' *Birds* was translated in the 19th century, the name of the realm built by the birds to separate the gods from mankind was called *Cloudcuckooland*, and this was then applied to any impossibly fanciful world. 'You're living in cloudcuckooland,' we might say. Later the expression was also used in a shortened form: *cuckoo land*. And in the 20th century, American English took this direction further: anyone who was thought to be crazy or making an absurd suggestion was, quite simply, *cuckoo*. And if you were thought to be seriously crazy, you might end up as Jack Nicholson did in the 1975 film, in a *cuckoo's nest*.

Cunt
a taboo word (13th century)

Taboo words are an important element in every language – not because of their number, but because of their notoriety. No other words attract such public emotions, headlines and legislation. But if a word-book is trying to represent all aspects of a language's lexicon, they have to be included. And they always provide a fascinating story, even if it is one which some readers may find uncomfortable in the telling.

Some studies suggest that the public is becoming more relaxed about traditional taboo words, but *cunt* remains at the top of any list of words that people find most offensive. It is one of a very few words known by their initials. The expression *the f-word* seems to have been the first, recorded since the 1950s. The *c-word* came later, in the 1970s. Today, such usages have extended to other kinds of taboo, such as race (the *n-word*, for *nigger*) and mortality (where *c-word* turns up again, but now standing for *cancer*).

Some taboo words, such as *bloody* (§47), emerge quite late in the history of English; others, such as *cunt*, seem to have been there very early on. But nobody knows exactly where this word came from or when it arrived. There's an Old Norse word *kunta* with the same meaning, so maybe it came in with the Vikings. It doesn't appear in Old English and is rare in Middle English, suggesting that it was a sensitive word even then. There are several instances of it being replaced by a less direct form (a euphemism), such as *quaint*, and other alternatives emerged, such as *cunny*, *quim* and the remarkable *quoniam* (the Latin word for 'since'), which must have originated as a scholarly joke. In Lichfield there is a street called

Quonians, which may well come from this source.

The story of *count* and *countess* is suggestive too. These aristocratic titles were brought over from France when the Normans arrived. But although *countess* was immediately adopted – there are examples recorded from the 12th century – *count* was not. Instead, the Anglo-Saxon word *earl* continued in use. The likely explanation is that *count* was being avoided because its pronunciation reminded people of *cunt*. The vowel in *count* would have been short (as shown by the early Old French spelling *cunte*). By the 16th century, though, things had changed: *count* was evidently being pronounced in a sufficiently different way for people to use it without causing a snigger, and the title becomes frequent thereafter. We find *Count Orsino, Count Claudio* and other *Counts* in Shakespeare.

On the other hand, the word evidently didn't have the same taboo force in the early Middle Ages that it has today. It turns up in various medical textbooks of the period, as a routine part of a description of female anatomy. It appears within surnames, such as *John Fillecunt* and *Bele Wydecunthe*. And there are some famous street names, such as *Gropecuntlane*, which suggest that the word was in common parlance. We won't find such names today. The old street names have long been replaced by more innocent versions. However, if you find yourself walking down a *Grope Street* or a *Grape Street*, it may well have once been a prostitution thoroughfare.

It took longer for the word to be used as a term of abuse. There are occasional signs in the 1500s of people using it when they were calling each other names, but the really forceful insulting use (*you cunt!*) isn't recorded until the early 20th century – first with reference to women, then to men as well – and chiefly in Britain. It's difficult to be sure when this usage began. Once *cunt* had achieved really strong taboo force, it became rare in writing, so we don't have any records. Dictionaries would generally exclude it. And when a few writers did dare to use it, it would usually be printed with a dash or asterisks.

Today, most dictionaries include it. But newspapers still vary in their practice. If a footballer calls a referee a cunt, which seems to happen quite often, we might see all three versions in different papers: *c---*, *c**** and *cunt*. Seeing the word in print at all is a major change compared with fifty years ago. But newspapers no longer dictate norms. If you want to see it used some 20 million or so times, all you have to do is call it up on the internet.

Wicked

a radical alteration (13th century)

When a word changes its meaning, it can sometimes take people by surprise, especially when the new meaning is very different from the old one. In the later decades of the 20th century, parents were taken aback when they heard their children start using *wicked* as a term of strong praise. In fact there was nothing especially unusual about the development. This wasn't the first time a word had taken on a meaning that was the opposite of its original sense.

Wicked emerged as an adjective during the 13th century. It seems to have come from the Old English word *wicca*, 'wizard' (and *wicce*, 'witch'), and from its earliest uses it had all the associations of evil and malignant supernatural powers. *The Wicked One* came to be a description of Satan, and any stock evil characters in plays would tend to attract the epithet. Pantomime today continues that tradition, with its *Wicked Fairy* and *Wicked Stepmother*.

Before long the word began to broaden its meaning, and was applied to all kinds of bad situations. Any cruel, fierce or vicious being, human or animal, could be called *wicked*. So could harmful, dangerous or offensive happenings. The air could be described as *wicked*, if it was foul-smelling; food also, if it was foul-tasting. A difficult road might be called *wicked*.

Then, towards the end of the 16th century, a lighter tone emerged. Someone might be described as having a *wicked tongue* or *wicked eyes*. Children were said to be *wicked imps*. Here the meaning is 'mischievous', 'sly' or 'naughty', and often the usage was distinctively jocular in tone. Later, people would even use the word to describe themselves in this way, adapting the biblical phrase (from the Book of Isaiah) to say *no peace/rest for the wicked!*

It was a short step from here to the 20th-century sense of 'amazing', 'splendid', 'remarkable' – a usage which is actually found in American slang as early as the 1920s. It's by no means alone. Other words which have developed the same set of laudatory senses include *sick, mad, insane* and *crazy*. The oddest, to my mind, is *horrorshow*. This was one of the words invented by Anthony Burgess in his novel *A Clockwork Orange*. It's a phonetic rendering of a Russian word meaning 'splendid', and that's how it has entered English slang. If someone were to say that 'this book was horrorshow', I'd really be rather pleased.

 ## *Wee*
a Scottish contribution (14th century)

In 1955, Frank Sinatra released an album called *In the Wee Small Hours*. Its title track – 'In the Wee Small Hours of the Morning' – was one of those songs that stay in the mind, and it's since been recorded by several other vocalists. But the expression wasn't a modern coinage. It has an ancient Scottish ancestry, and represents an important strand in the history of English.

Wee had travelled a long way by the time it reached the Hollywood recording studios. We first find it in the north of England in the 1300s, in such phrases as *a little wee*, and it soon moved up into Scotland. It could mean several things – 'a little child', 'a small

FRANK SINATRA

in the **wee small hours**

The cover of the 1955 record album by Frank Sinatra. The nursery rhyme 'ee Willie Winkie' has done a great deal to popularise the word among 1-Scottish children.

quantity' or 'a short distance or period of time'. The senses were all to do with the 'amount' of something. There's a relationship with the Old English word *weigh*.

Eventually *wee* became an adjective meaning 'extremely small', 'tiny'. And often it was used in a more general sense: 'little'. A *wee bairn* was just a 'small child'. Then an interesting development took place: *wee* became a term of endearment – a friendly, welcoming word – and began to lose its association with size. That's how it's often used today. If someone in Scotland invites you for *a wee drink*, beware! It won't necessarily be a small one.

Scottish English emerged as a really distinctive dialect of the language very early on. It all began when English loyalists fled to Scotland after the Norman Conquest in 1066. They were made welcome there, and by the 13th century English had become the dominant language of the lowland south and east. Then, in 1296, Edward I of England invaded Scotland – the start of a 300-years war. It's hardly surprising, accordingly, that with Scots identity at stake the English language would soon evolve a local character, quite unlike anything south of the River Tweed.

And it certainly did. Today, Scots English is alive and well, heard and seen in a variety of dialects, and with a local vocabulary of thousands of words, such as *gang* ('go'), *richt* ('right'), *bonnie* ('pretty') and *mickle* ('great'). Some of the words and phrases have travelled well outside Scotland, as *wee* illustrates. But the prize for the most famous and well-travelled Scots expression has surely got to go to *Auld Lang Syne* – the Robert Burns poem sung traditionally at New Year. It literally means 'old long since' – that is, 'for old times' sake'. The words and tune have attracted the singers too, such as Billy Joel and Bobby Darin, and they've appeared in dozens of films. Not a bad result, for a British regional dialect.

Grammar
a surprising link (14th century)

Grammar is glamorous? For many people, that would be an impossible association of ideas, remembering a time when they were taught English grammar in school, trying to analyse complicated sentences into parts, and learning rules and terms whose purpose was never clear. Glamorous it wasn't. For others, the association would be pointless, for they were never taught any English grammar at all.

This was a great shame, as grammar, when taught properly, is indeed an exciting and stimulating subject. It's the study of the way we compose our sentences, of how we say what we mean and of the different effects we convey by varying the order of our words. In short, grammar shows us how we make sense. And the more we know about grammar, the more we understand how language works.

But this book isn't about grammatical constructions; it's about words. And when we explore the origins of the word *grammar*, we find some real surprises. Would you expect an encounter with magic and the supernatural? Read on.

Grammar comes from a Latin word, *grammatica*, which in turn derives from *gramma*, meaning a written mark, or letter. It originally included the study of everything that was written – literature as well as language – and eventually this sense was extended to mean the knowledge that a person acquires through literacy. But people who could read and write were an élite. They included not only monks and scholars but also those who dealt in astrology and magic. This is where the supernatural comes in. In medieval Europe, the word *grammar* was often used to talk about the study of the occult. And when the word arrived in English, in the 14th century, it brought in those associations. A new word emerged: people would talk about *gramarye*, meaning 'occult learning', 'necromancy'.

It's this magical sense that leads to *glamour*. In the 18th century in Scotland, people took up the word *grammar*, meaning 'an enchantment' or 'a spell', but they changed the pronunciation. Devils and wizards were said to *cast the glamour* over the eyes of onlookers. From here it was a short step to the meaning of an alluring charm surrounding someone or something. And in the 20th century, we see the word arriving at its present-day sense of 'charm' and 'attractiveness'.

In the 1930s, people talked about *glamour boys* – a phrase given popular appeal when it was used to describe the handsome young airmen of the wartime RAF. Eventually the adjective came to be used chiefly for women, especially after the movies popularised the phrase *glamour girls*, and the pin-up photograph became widespread.

The word took an unexpected direction in the 1950s, when it began to be used as a euphemism for nude or topless modelling. If you were offered *glamour photographs*, you wouldn't expect to see much clothing. Girls, such as those gracing page 3 in *The Sun* newspaper, were described as *glamour models*, and the agencies and events promoting them were said to be on the *glamour circuit*. The term is still widely used in this way.

The unexpected link between *grammar* and *glamour* illustrates a general point about the history of words. Often, a source word develops meanings that are so different from each other that we don't suspect they have a common origin. Who would ever guess that there's a common origin for *salary, sausage, sauce* and *salad*? And who would ever have predicted that *grammar* would one day give birth to such a flamboyant and publicity-seeking child as *glamour*? *Grammar* hasn't yet achieved such a vivid popular presence – but I live in hope.

28 *Valentine*
first name into word (14th century)

On 14 February each year, in many countries, people send valentines as love tokens – usually a card, flowers or a small gift. Often it's a chance for one person to express secret admiration for another. People sometimes spend ages deciding what to send and whether they ought to send it. But they probably don't spend a moment reflecting on the linguistic character of what it is they're sending.

Valentine is an example of a first name being used as a common noun. The practice is surprisingly common, though many of the uses are specialised or slang. Certain kinds of apples, pears, daisies, magpies and fish have all at some time or other been called *Margaret*. Certain kinds of flags (*Blue Peter*) and card tricks (in whist or bridge) have been called *Peter* – as have cash registers, prison cells and penises.

Sometimes the name becomes part of a generally used idiom. People talk about *a Jack of all trades, simple Simon, a proper Charlie, taking the Mickey* and *every Tom, Dick or Harry*. In Australian English, *Sheila* is used colloquially for a young woman and *John* for a policeman (from French *gendarme* – 'johndarm'). *John* can be a lavatory in American English. Literature provides examples too, such as a *Sherlock* for a detective or a *Lolita* for a sexually precocious young girl. And the Bible has given us an *Adam* for a gardener, a *Samson* for a strong man and a *Solomon* for a wise man. Named disasters can travel too: 'We don't want to see another (hurricane) Katrina.'

In many of these cases, we have no idea who the source person was. Charlie may well have been Charlie Chaplin, but who was the original Jack or Sheila? Nobody knows. And *Valentine* presents a puzzle too. The feast day of 14 February commemorates two early Christian martyrs from Italy, both named Valentine. But neither of them seems to have had any obvious link with romantic love. The amorous associations first come to the fore in Geoffrey Chaucer's poem 'The Parliament of Fowls', written in the early 1380s, telling the story of Nature convening an assembly where the birds choose their mates.

Humans evidently rather liked the idea, because quite soon we find a variety of activities associated with the day. A common practice was a valentine lottery: names would be written on folded pieces of paper and placed in a pot, and the pairings which were drawn out would motivate a special relationship for the coming year. As a result, the papers themselves came to be called *valentines*, and this led to the practice of sending paper valentines and then valentine cards. In the 19th century it became big business, with manufacturers producing highly ornate creations, adorned with lace and ribbons. Children would go from house to house on the day, asking for small gifts. The practice was called *valentining*.

But we can never predict the course of language

change, and eventually senses of *valentine* developed where the romantic associations of the word were left far behind. In the 16th century, a sealed letter from the Crown to landholders demanding the arrest of lawbreakers came to be called a *valentine*. And in the Second World War the name was given to a 16-ton heavy infantry tank. Why? Its production was apparently given the go-ahead on 14 February 1938.

 ## 29 *Egg*
a dialect choice (14th century)

One of the most famous words in the history of English language studies is *eggs*. It's all because of William Caxton, who introduced printing to England in 1476.

Caxton was faced with a real problem. For hundreds of years, English had been written down by scribes from different parts of the country with different kinds of training. There was a huge variation in the way words were spelled. A word like *might* appears in manuscripts in over thirty different spellings – *micht*, *mycht*, *myght*, *mihte* and so on. Caxton had to make a choice. Which one was most likely to be most widely understood?

It wasn't just spelling that posed a problem. People from different parts of the country used different words for the same thing – dialect variations. And this is where *eggs* comes in. In the prologue to one of the books Caxton printed, he tells a story he had heard about a shipful of sailors who were becalmed in the Thames estuary, and who decided to make a shore visit while they waited for the wind to pick up. One of them went into a café (as we'd call it today) and asked for some 'eggs', but the lady who ran the establishment didn't understand what he wanted, and replied that she couldn't speak French. This made the sailor angry, because he couldn't speak French either! He just wanted 'eggs'. Then someone else told the lady that what the sailor actually wanted was 'eyren'. She understood that, so the sailor got his eggs.

This story sums up Caxton's confusion. 'Lo!', he says, 'what should a man in these days now write, eggs or eyren?' And he goes on: 'It's hard to please every man because of diversity and change in language.' He would have to choose one or other of these words, if he were printing a text about eggs, and which one should he go for? He was a businessman, not a linguist, and he was – understandably – confused.

Why were there two words? *Eggs* was a word used chiefly in the north of England at the time. It was an Old Norse word, presumably brought to England by the Viking invaders a few hundred years earlier, though it doesn't appear in writing until the 14th century. *Eyren* was used in the south of England – a development of the word that the Anglo-Saxons had used. Eventually, as we now know, *eyren* died out and *eggs* became the word in everyday use.

We don't know whether the café owner was serious, or whether she was having a joke at the expense of the hungry sailor. But the tale does illustrate well the way people were beginning to feel the need for a kind of English that would be understood throughout the country. In the *egg* story we see one of the origins of present-day standard English.

30 *Royal*
word triplets (14th century)

Monarchs couldn't have been *regal* or *royal* in Anglo-Saxon times. They could only have been *king-like* or *queen-like*. But during the 14th century, as part of the huge influx of vocabulary into English from French and Latin, *regal* and *royal* arrived, and along with *kingly/queenly* made up a cluster of words that have, rather sweetly, been called *triplets*.

Why did English speakers welcome these new words? All three basically mean 'king/queen-like', after all. Why have three words when one might do? The answer reveals something of the character of the language, for this triplet is not alone. We see the same sort of development taking place repeatedly, such as with Germanic *ask*, French *question* and Latin *interrogate*; Germanic *fire*, French *flame* and Latin *conflagration*; and Germanic *holy*, French *sacred* and Latin *consecrated*. As the examples build up, we can begin to see a pattern. The Germanic words are short and feel down-to-earth; the Latin words are long and scholarly; and the French words have a different set of associations.

It's sometimes said that we know a word by the company it keeps. From the very beginning, *regal* and *royal* went in different directions. *Regal* went conceptual, used with such 'authority' words as *throne, government* and *power*, as well as 'appearance' words such as *demeanour, figure* and *look*. *Royal* went personal, used with 'ancestry' words such as *blood, birth* and *family*, as well as 'position' words such as *princess, majesty* and *highness*. Learnèd Latin offered an alternative mode of expression to courtly French, and both were more stately, refined and cultured than their Anglo-Saxon equivalents.

These trends are still apparent today. *Regal* has had relatively little development over the centuries. It still typically adds connotations of superiority or distinction. Anything *regal*, by implication, is 'fit for royalty' – hence its application to such things as cars (*Buick Regal*), whisky (*Chivas Regal*), buildings (*Regal Cinema*) and the visit from an especially magisterial great-aunt.

By contrast, *royal* has accumulated a huge range of uses. It's used in relation to the activities and words of royal people (*royal charter, visit, assent, command, warrant* and not forgetting the *royal we* – 'We are not amused') as well as social groups (*Royal Navy, Borough, Society*) and a host of person-related activities such as transport (*Royal Scot*), colours (*royal blue*) and cards (*royal flush*).

The words don't substitute for each other. The *Royal Mail* could not become the *Regal Mail* or the *Queenly Mail*. Nor is it possible, except in jest, to talk about the *Regal Shakespeare Company* or the *Kingly Albert Hall*. *Kingly* and *queenly* seem to be dying out, in fact, with only a few hundred thousand hits on Google, whereas *regal* has 20 million and *royal* 200 million.

But we can never predict the future, when it comes to vocabulary. Who would ever have thought, in the Middle Ages, that *royal* would one day be used as a colloquial intensifier, similar to *bloody*? But it happened in the 19th century, and the usage is still with us. I recently heard someone say *He's a royal pain in the neck*. And the defeat of a local football enemy was summed up in the regal words: *They got a right royal hammering*.

 ## Money
a productive idiom (14th century)

Vocabulary isn't just a matter of single words. It includes thousands of idioms – strings of words which have taken on a special meaning. We talk about doing something *at the drop of a hat* ('immediately'), *getting cold feet* ('becoming afraid') and having *a heart of gold* ('a generous nature'). Some words are very frequently used in idioms. *Money* is one of them – a popular idiomatic source since the word arrived from French in the 14th century.

You can give someone *a run for their money, see the colour of their money, get your money's worth, have money to burn* and *spend money like water.* Maybe you won't do something *for love nor money,* perhaps because you're *not made of money.* Or maybe you will, because it's *money for old rope, money for jam.* If you've got some, then *money is no object* and it might *burn a hole in your pocket.* You can *put your money where your mouth is. Money talks,* after all. And if you're feeling proverbial, you can observe that *money is the root of all evil, doesn't grow on trees* and *makes the world go round.* Even non-standard grammar can survive in standard English as an idiom. *You pays your money and you takes your choice.*

It's not just the general word that attracts idioms. The individual coins and banknotes do too, reflecting the currency of the culture. So in American English people *feel like a million dollars, make a fast buck, bet their bottom dollar* and *put their two cents worth* into a conversation. Some, such as *pass the buck,* have become part of colloquial standard English everywhere. In other cases, the idiom is translated: in British English, we're more likely to see *feel like a million quid* and *put in their two pence worth.*

If there's a change in the currency system, or in the value of money, it quickly affects the language (§86). *Penny* and *pence* have been really popular over the centuries, but many of these idiomatic expressions reflect an age when things cost a penny. In old publications we'll find such expressions as *penny dreadful, penny bun, penny bank, penny arcade, penny*

7. The 19th-century Yorkshire Penny Bank building in Bradford, West Yorkshire, UK. The idea behind the name was that savings could be deposited as small as a penny – a practice that the larger banks did not condone.

whistle and *penny novelette*. Some live on. Many people still say that cheap things are *ten a penny*, observe that something expensive is *a pretty penny* and offer others *a penny for your thoughts*. And, even in an age of new technology, people still say *the penny dropped*, from the 1930s, when people put a penny in a slot machine. Older people still use the euphemism about going *to spend a penny*, though the days when a public lavatory had a penny slot are long gone. Today it costs at least 20p, and more in some places. Maybe one day British English will get a new idiom: *I have to spend a pound*.

Music

a spelling in evolution (14th century)

How many possible ways are there to spell *music*? Today, just one. But over the history of English we see this word spelled in over forty ways. The word arrived from French in the 14th century, and early spellings reflected its origins. We find the French *q* in such forms as *musiqe*, *musyque* and *musique*. An English *k* makes its appearance in *musyk*, *musik* and *musike*. A few writers opted for *c*, producing *musice* and *music*.

The uncertainty led to some strange combinations. In the 15th century we find *musycque*, *mewsycke*, *musick*, *musicke* and others. And in the 16th century some writers, evidently totally at a loss, decided to cover themselves by using all three consonants: *musickque*. The vowels too were variable, especially when people pronounced the word in different ways. We find *moosick, mwsick, maisick, masic, meesic* and *misic*.

When Dr Johnson published his *Dictionary*, in 1755, most of these variations had disappeared, but the modern spelling had not yet arrived. Johnson had strong views about spelling, and was of the opinion that 'The English never use *c* at the end of a word'. So in his dictionary we find *musick*, as well as *comick*, *critick, physick, publickly* and many others. But this is one of those occasions where Dr Johnson's authority wasn't enough. In the USA, Noah Webster and other dictionary writers began dropping the final *k* as part of the changes being introduced into American English. The change evidently had universal appeal, for within a few decades the final *k* had been dropped from these words in British English too.

There is still a great deal of variation in the spelling of English words. Some of it is due to the differences between British and American English, such as *colour* and *color* or *litre* and *liter*. Some is due to different printing traditions, such as *judgment* and *judgement* or *organise* and *organize*. There is still a great deal of variation over whether to insert a hyphen or not in such words as *washing machine* and *flower pot*. And the situation remains fluid, with American spellings increasingly influencing British ones. Words such as *encyclopaedia, paediatrics* and *archaeology* are often now seen as *encyclopedia, pediatrics* and *archeology* on both sides of the Atlantic, and around the Pacific too. And probably we ain't seen nothin' yet. The internet is likely to eliminate some of the irregular spellings that have crept into English over the centuries.

When *rhubarb* came into English in the 14th century, it had no *h*: it had such spellings as *rubarb* and *rewbarb*. The *h* was added much later by writers who wanted to show the classical origins of the word. Today, people are voting with their fingers. Type *rubarb* into Google and you will get 80,000 hits (in 2011). And in fifty years' time? Maybe *rhubarb* by then will seem as archaic as *Ye Olde Tea Shoppe* does now.

Taffeta
an early trade word (14th century)

On 14 July 1724 a fleet of cargo ships arrived in England after the long journey from the East Indies, carrying goods on behalf of the United Company of Merchants. The cargo lists showed *1846 addaties, 1279 alliballies* and *1997 baftaes*, and the rest of the cargo included various numbers of *carridarries, chillaes, cushtaes, doofooties, emerties, ginghams, lacowries, nillaes, romals* and *taffeties*.

How many of these words do you know? Most people recognise *ginghams*, and might be able to identify some of the others if they really know the history of fabrics. But for most of us, the terms have no reality other than to provide ammunition for word-guessing games such as *Fictionary* or *Call My Bluff*. In fact they are all types of cotton, linen or silk, with names reflecting local Indian usage, or sometimes the town of origin (as with *cushtaes*, from Kushtia in Bangladesh). A few names refer to types of product, such as *romals*, which were silk or cotton squares or handkerchiefs.

We tend to underestimate the importance of words like these in the history of English vocabulary because they are so specialised. Few of them ever get into general dictionaries. But, for a language like English, in a country like Britain, tens of thousands of words have entered the language as a result of global trade. Many of them, such as *calico*, *chintz* and *khaki*, retain a distinctive spelling reflecting their exotic origins.

Taffeta is first recorded in 1373. It appears in the list above as *taffetie* – one of many recorded spellings of the word before it settled down in its modern form. Its meaning has varied over the centuries, referring to various kinds of fabric, but its primary application has been to silk of a rich and lustrous quality. This led to *taffeta* being extended to non-fabric situations. Anything ornate or florid might be described in this way. Shakespeare has one of his characters, Berowne in *Love's Labour's Lost* (V.ii.406), say how he will never woo a lady in artificial 'silken terms'. He calls them 'taffeta phrases'.

Taffeta is ultimately from Persian, a language we don't normally think of as a source for English vocabulary; but over the years, either directly or indirectly, it has supplied English with a surprising number of words (§48). You are entering an originally Persian linguistic world if you ever find yourself sitting on a *divan* in a *caravan*, wearing a *scarlet* or *lilac shawl*, eating *couscous*, having been *checkmated* by a *rook* in *chess* and watching 'The Day of the *Jackal*'. The shawl would have to be taffeta, of course.

Information(s)

34

(un)countable nouns (14th century)

It's one of the commonest errors heard when people are learning English as a foreign language. They say such things as 'I want to buy some furnitures', 'I'd like some advices' and 'Do you have any informations about that?' Or they use the singular form, and talk about *a furniture, an advice, an information.*

Teachers know why such things happen. It's often interference from the student's mother tongue. In French, for example, *information* is used as a plural when it means 'news', so French learners assume the same thing happens in English. Teachers sort it out by getting learners to say *a piece of information,* and suchlike. And they draw attention to the important distinction between nouns that are *countable* in English (such as *eggs, chairs* and *elephants*) and those that aren't – *uncountable* nouns such as *information*.

However, we mustn't fall into the trap of thinking that words like these can never vary. In fact, when *information* arrived in English from French in the 14th century, it was also used as a countable noun, with the meaning of 'a charge' or 'accusation'. Someone might *make informations* about you. And in law, this countable usage remains today in various technical senses.

It was used as a countable noun in everyday English too, in the sense of 'a piece of advice' or 'a piece of news'. Chaucer talks about *wise informations and teachings*. Coverdale's Bible has *informations and documents of wisdom*. And usages such as *reliable informations* and *latest informations* can be found in print written by native speakers right up to the present day. At the same time as all this was going on, of course, *information* was developing its uncountable use, which is the most common use today in this *information age*.

The message is plain. Words can be countable or uncountable depending on the sense we have in mind when we use them. Before the 20th century, *tea* and *coffee* were uncountable, apart from in specialist settings where types of tea or coffee were being identified. But in recent times we have seen the development from 'Would you like tea/coffee?' to 'Would you like a cup of tea/coffee?' to 'Would you like a tea/coffee?' and such usages as 'Two teas/coffees, please'. We also say 'I like tea/coffee' and

'Would you like some tea/coffee'. These words have two uses today.

Many words switch in this way. We eat *cake* and *a cake*. We play *piano* and *a piano*. We hear *noise* and *a noise*. We turn on *a light* to let some *light* in. The process works the other way round too. Countable nouns can become uncountable. I can imagine a children's story about a family of moths discussing what they're going to have for lunch today. 'I'm eating coat', says one. 'I tried some coat yesterday, and it wasn't very nice', says another, 'I prefer hat, personally'. Well, why not?

Gaggle
a collective noun (15th century)

I think it went something like this. A group of monks, wondering how to pass the time on a cold, dark winter's evening in the 15th century, invent a word game. 'Let's think up words for groups of things', says one. 'What do we call a group of cows?' 'A herd.' 'A group of bees?' 'A swarm.' 'A group of geese?' 'A flock.' Words like *herd* and *swarm* had been in the language since Anglo-Saxon times. There weren't many of them, and the few that were available had been used for all kinds of things. People talked about a *herd of cranes, wrens, deer, swans, gnats* and more. The game must have palled after a while.

Then someone had a bright idea. 'Let's think up

better words. What would be a really clever way of talking about geese?' 'A cackle of geese, maybe?' 'Not bad, but that better suits hens. What about *gaggle*? It goes better with goose because of the *g*'s? What do you all think?' 'Agreed? Write it down, Brother John.'

And Brother John did. Or maybe it was Dame Juliana. She was the prioress of Sopwell nunnery, near St Albans in Hertfordshire, and her name appears in a collection of material on hunting, heraldry and folklore that was printed in 1486, called *The Book of St Albans*. It's one of the first English printed books, and it contains a list of some 200 collective nouns. Several are traditional expressions, such as *herd*. But many seem to be inventions. This is where we find *a muster of peacocks, an unkindness of ravens, a watch of nightingales, a charm of goldfinches* and dozens more. But the list goes well beyond animals. We find *a diligence of messengers, a superfluity of nuns, a doctrine of doctors, a sentence of judges, a prudence of vicars* and *a non-patience of wives*. And people tried out fresh combinations. 'A gaggle of geese?' 'What about a gaggle of women?' 'Write that down, Brother John.' He did. A *gaggle of women* is recorded in a book written around 1470. An early sexist joke.

Why do I think this is the sort of thing that happened? Because this is a game people still happily play today, and human nature hasn't changed that much in 500 years. A great deal of entertainment can be derived from thinking up the funniest way of describing a group of 'X' – where X can be anything from dog handlers to dentists. What's the best collective noun for politicians, or undertakers, or linguists? Competitions have produced some fine examples. I made my own collection a few years ago, and found many that deserve prizes. Here's a top ten:

> An absence of waiters
> A rash of dermatologists
> A shoulder of agony aunts
> A clutch of car mechanics
> A vat of chancellors
> A bout of estimates
> A lot of auctioneers
> A mass of priests
> A whored of prostitutes
> A depression of weather forecasters
> An exces's of apostrophes

And still they come. In recent times I've encountered *a crash of software, an annoyance of mobile phones* and *a bond of British secret agents*.

 ## *Doable*
a mixing of languages (15th century)

How many English words do you know? People tend to seriously underestimate the size of their personal vocabulary. They think that it's only a few thousand words. But if you were to take a dictionary and work your way through, ticking the words you know, you'd be pleasantly surprised. The total would be at least 50,000.

This figure seems less surprising when we reflect on how easy it is to make up new words. A single word can generate a whole family. *Happy, happily, happiness, unhappy, unhappily, unhappiness, happy-go-lucky, happy-hour, happy-dust, happy-hearted, happy-clappy, trigger-happy, slap-happy* ... The prefixes (such as *un-*) and the suffixes (such as *-ly* and *-ness*) are especially important in building up our vocabulary. There are just over a hundred of them in everyday English, and at least one will be found in nearly half the words in the language. Most of them came in from Latin and French during the Middle Ages. That's when we find a flood of new words beginning with such forms as *con-, de-, dis-* and *ex-*, and ending with such forms as *-ment, -tion, -ity* and *-able*.

The French suffix *-able* alone produced hundreds of words. It was immediately used not only with French loanwords, such as *agreeable* and *changeable*, but also with Old English words to produce such forms as *knowable* and *doable*. *Doable*, first recorded in the mid-1400s, is a good choice to represent the class. *Do* is one of the earliest known English verbs, found in some of the first Anglo-Saxon texts, and here it is happily being used with a French suffix. It shows that word-coiners are no respecter of origins.

Another flood of creations began when *un-* started to be used with *-able* words, in the 14th century, so we get *unknowable, unthinkable* and many more. Then a remarkable thing happened. The *-able* was added to two-element verbs. We find *get-at-able* and *come-at-able*, and then *unget-at-able* and *uncome-at-able*. Some writers went over the top. Ben Jonson coined *un-in-one-breath-utterable*. But the basic pattern became very popular. Since the 12th century there have been hundreds of coinages, such as *undryupable* and *unkeepoff-able*. Not all have achieved a permanent place in the language, but some, such as *unputdownable, unswitchoffable* and *unwearoutable,* are often used. And a few have developed their own linguistic families. What is the state or quality of 'being get-at-able'? The 19th century provided the answer. *Get-at-ability. Get-at-ableness.*

Matrix
a word from Tyndale (16th century)

Ask most young people what *matrix* means and they will tell you. It is the name of the computer-simulated reality which will imprison the minds of human beings in the not-so-distant future, and it has a capital *M*. They are thinking of the 1999 science-fiction action film starring Keanu Reeves. This is as far away from the Bible as it is possible to get, but the link is there, linguistically. For the first clear use of the word *matrix* is in an English translation of the Gospel of St Luke (2: 23) made in 1525 by William Tyndale.

It's often said that no single book has had greater influence on the vocabulary of the English language than the Bible. I don't dispute that, as long as by 'Bible' we mean all the English translations that have been made, starting with John Wycliffe's manuscript version in about 1382 and ending with the King James Bible of 1611. The King James text is usually cited as the main influence, and in a way it was, as its official status meant that it would be heard and read by more people in Britain than any previous translation. But its main role was to popularise. Most of the words and phrases that would become part of everyday English had already been introduced by earlier translations – and by Tyndale, in particular. Think of *let there be light, am I my brother's keeper?, let my people go, the powers that be, the signs of the times* and *eat, drink and be merry.* These are all Tyndale.

In vocabulary he was extremely conservative, as were most Bible translators. He wanted his translation to be understood by the ordinary person rather than the theologian, so he went in for everyday words, and hardly ever coined words himself. Only 120 entries in the *Oxford English Dictionary* have a first recorded use attributed to him. They include several compound words, such as *busybody, castaway, broken-hearted, long-suffering* and *stumbling-block,* as well as *childishness, excommunicate, ungodliness* – and *matrix.*

Matrix has had an interesting history. It originates in the Latin word for 'mother', *mater.* Tyndale uses it to mean a 'womb', which was one of its meanings in Latin. By the 16th century the sense had broadened to mean a place where something begins; by the 18th century, the structure or material in which something is embedded; and by the 19th century, the elements which make up that something, seen as a network. People started applying the term to social networks, talking about a *political matrix*, for example. And in the mid-20th century it started to be used in the business world: an organisation in which communication operates through a web of relationships was said to illustrate *matrix management*.

Meanwhile, various technologies had adopted the term. Dentists used it to describe the material which serves as a temporary wall for a cavity when filling a tooth. Photographers used it as part of their printing process. Printers used it to describe the mould in which a piece of metal type was cast. Electronic engineers used it to talk about a type of circuit. And in 1990s' computing, *the matrix* became a popular term for the global network of electronic communication.

The stage was set for Keanu Reeves. Here we have a word which at one level means an organisational network and at another level means the electronic network that makes up cyberspace. It was only a matter of time before it would be picked up by the science-fiction world. And *time* is the relevant word, as the first recorded use of *matrix* in this genre is in a 1976 episode of *Dr Who*.

38 *Alphabet*
talking about writing (16th century)

When it comes to talking about the English language, no word holds a more central place in the popular mind than *alphabet*. Although speech long preceded writing in the history of language, and children learn to speak years before they learn to write, we find we can talk about letters more easily than we can talk about sounds. Letters are nice distinct shapes, and each shape has a simple name which we probably learned at our mother's knee – A, B, C ... Sounds are not so easy to identify, and – unless we've learned to transcribe them using a phonetic alphabet – not so easy to name.

So it can come as a bit of a surprise to learn that the word *alphabet* arrives in English quite late – almost a thousand years after the language was first written down. It's first used during the 16th century, at a time when thousands of new words were being borrowed from Latin and Greek to make the language, as the historian William Camden put it, 'beautified and enriched'. And many of these new words allowed people to talk more efficiently about what they were doing when they were speaking and writing. Think of all the words we have today to describe punctuation marks, for example, such as *comma* and *full stop*. Most were first used during the 1500s. And *alphabet* was one of them, first recorded in a 1580 dictionary.

We're so used to the idea of an alphabet nowadays that it's difficult to imagine a time when the notion wasn't a routine part of everyday life. Once we've learned to read, we don't think twice about putting things into alphabetical order, and we expect words to be in order when we look them up in telephone directories, indexes and so on. But in 1604, when Robert Cawdrey published the first English dictionary, he felt it was such a new idea that he had to explain in his introduction how his 'Table Alphabeticall' should be used:

> If thou be desirous (gentle Reader) rightly and readily to understand, and to profit by this Table, and such like, then thou must learn the alphabet, to wit, the order of the Letters as they stand, perfectly without book, and where every Letter standeth: as *b* near the beginning, *n* about the middest, and *t* toward the end.

In Shakespeare's time, children had a hornbook to help them learn their letters. This was a handheld device looking a bit like a long-handled mirror, but displaying a sheet on which was printed the alphabet in large and small letters, along with a small selection of other reading material. The sheet was usually covered by a thin layer of translucent horn, hence its name.

By the 18th century, alphabet books were arriving in schools, and soon they were all the rage. The writers looked for new ways of making the learning of letters appeal to a young readership. Authors and illustrators began to play with the language, using alliteration and rhyme. Stories were told about Angry Alice, Timid Tabitha and a host of other characters.

8. A typical children's hornbook from the 16th century.

Alphabet games appealed to the adult reader too. The most famous one was written by a journalist, Alaric Watts, which first appeared in the *Trifler* magazine in 1817. It has been reprinted thousands of times, often with variations.

An Austrian army, awfully arrayed,
Boldly by battery besieged Belgrade.
Cossack commanders cannonading come,
Dealing destruction's devastating doom.
Every endeavour engineers essay,
For fame, for fortune fighting – furious fray!
Generals 'gainst generals grapple – gracious God!
How honours Heaven heroic hardihood!
Infuriate, indiscriminate in ill,
Kindred kill kinsmen, kinsmen kindred kill.
Labour low levels longest, loftiest lines;
Men march 'mid mounds, 'mid moles, 'mid
    murderous mines;
Now noxious, noisy numbers nothing, naught
Of outward obstacles, opposing ought;
Poor patriots, partly purchased, partly pressed,
Quite quaking, quickly 'Quarter! Quarter!' quest.
Reason returns, religious right redounds,
Suwarrow stops such sanguinary sounds.
Truce to thee, Turkey! Triumph to thy train,
Unwise, unjust, unmerciful Ukraine!
Vanish vain victory! vanish, victory vain!
Why wish we warfare? Wherefore welcome were
Xerxes, Ximenes, Xanthus, Xavier?
Yield, yield, ye youths! ye yeomen, yield your yell!
Zeus', Zarpater's, Zoroaster's zeal,
Attracting all, arms against acts appeal!

Suwarrow, incidentally, was the name of a Russian general. And did you notice that there was no line for *J*? This was because *J* was seen as a variant of *I*.

Alphabet achieved new heights in the 20th century, when its use was extended by computer scientists to include numerals and other characters. It also became one of the few words which we could literally eat. Around 1900, food manufacturers introduced a clear soup containing tiny pieces of pasta or biscuit shaped like individual letters. They called it *alphabet soup*. And not long after there was *alphabetti spaghetti*.

39 *Potato*
a European import (16th century)

Something very noticeable happened to English vocabulary during the 16th and 17th centuries. It began to look different. Loanwords from French had already started the process in the early Middle Ages. New French words meant new French spellings. But the revival of learning known as the Renaissance brought a fresh encounter with the countries of Europe, and as the people of Britain learned about the latest thing in such areas as science, architecture, cuisine and the arts, so they found themselves faced with an array of new words and spellings that must have seemed bizarre.

Bizarre was one. *Grotesque* was another. These

were from French. So were *moustache, colonel, vogue* and *naive*. Even less familiar would have been the way words were ending with sounded vowels. English had long had a 'silent *e*', usually marking a long vowel earlier in a word (*house, time, sore* ...), but a sounded final *-ee* in a word of several syllables was a novelty, as in *devotee, referee* and *repartee*.

A final *-o* in these new loanwords must have felt really strange. Italian imports included *cameo, concerto, portico, soprano* and *volcano*. Spanish or Portuguese arrivals included *bravado, desperado, mosquito, tobacco* and *potato*. Some of these words originated in the Indian languages of South or Central America. *Potato* is one of them, thought to be from a Haitian language, and introduced to Spain by Christopher Columbus.

Words like *potato* presented a number of linguistic problems. People were evidently uncomfortable with the *-o* ending, for a popular early spelling was *potatoe*. And then, how should they turn it into a plural? Simply 'adding an *s*', which is the usual English way, would give *potatos*, and that *-os* ending didn't well reflect the long vowel. *Potatoes,* as we now know, became the standard spelling. But in the 16th century, there was an alternative solution: use an apostrophe. We find *potato's* – one of the earliest examples of what today some people call the 'greengrocer's apostrophe'. The problem didn't go away. English speakers have never felt comfortable with the spelling of words ending in sounded vowels, which is why forms such as *potato's* and *tomato's* are still widely seen.

Spelling aside, *potato* has been quite a linguistic success story. Few vegetables have acquired such a wide range of meanings. In the 18th century, unimportant or worthless things or people began to be called *potatoes*. The poet Samuel Taylor Coleridge once famously described the London literati as *little potatoes*. American English began to use the phrase *small potatoes* for something unimportant. Then there was a curious development: *potato* developed the opposite sense. Now it meant something or someone was right, correct, excellent. *That's the potato!* In Australian English we find *clean potato* being used for a first-rate or honest person. And American slang gave us a sense of 'money': *Got the potatoes to buy it?*

A really odd development was when the word came to be used in a children's counting game. *One potato, two potato, three potato, four ...* – linguistically highly unusual because there's no plural ending. And something even odder happened in Australian slang, when in the mid-20th century *potato* came to be used as a slang word for a girl or woman. Why? Rhyming slang. *Potato peeler*. Sheila.

10 *Debt*

a spelling reform (16th century)

Why on earth is there a *b* in *debt*? This is one of the questions that English learners – native speakers and foreigners alike, faced with yet another irregular spelling to be acquired – ask with a mixture of frustration and resignation. 'The language seems to have gone out of its way to make things difficult,' said a student to me once. That's certainly how it appears. Except we have to remember that language has no existence outside of the people who use it. And it is people who put the *b* into *debt*.

Sixteenth-century people, to be exact. That was a century when writers were hugely expanding the language through the use of loanwords, as we saw with words like *potato* (**§39**), and Latin and Greek were especially favoured because of their prestige in literature and education. Many writers felt that English would become a much better medium, capable of reaching the heights achieved by the classical languages, if it used as many Latin and Greek words as possible. And the more these words looked like classical words, the better.

Debt, meaning 'something owed', had been in English since around 1300. It was a French word, and in French it was spelled *dete* or *dette*. So English did the same, using those spellings as well as *det* and *dett*. Here we have a neat phonetic representation of how the word sounded. Why would anyone ever want to change it?

A good question. But the mindset of the 16th century was different. Scholars pointed out that the ultimate origin of the word was Latin, not French, and in Latin the word was *debitum*. So writers made the word 'look' more classical by introducing a *b*, and the practice caught on. It was reinforced by other loanwords where the Latin consonant was pronounced, such as *debit* and *dubious*.

Debt was not alone. The same process affected *doubt*, which came into English spelled *dute* or *doute*, and a *b* was added because people remembered Latin *dubitare*. *Subtle* got its *b* from Latin *subtilis*, though earlier it had such spellings as *sotill* and *suttell*. *Receipt* got its *p* from Latin *recepta*, despite earlier spellings such as *recyt* and *resseit*. Baptism came in as *baptem* or *baptime*, then acquired an *s* from Latin *baptismus*. *Fault* came in as *faut* or *faute*, then added an *l* from Latin *fallita*. There were many more.

Of course, once a word was spelled in a certain way, some people then thought that all the letters should be pronounced. The pedantic schoolteacher Holofernes, in Shakespeare's *Love's Labour's Lost* (V.i.20), is horrified at the thought that there are people who *don't* pronounce the *b* in *debt*! In fact, few of these Latin letters ever came to be pronounced, except in jest. *Baptism* was an exception. So was *fault*. We pronounce the *l* today, but even in the 18th century the word was being pronounced 'faut'. Dr Johnson tells us in his *Dictionary*: 'The *l* is sometimes sounded, and sometimes mute. In conversation it is generally suppressed.' And his quotations from Pope and Dryden show it rhyming with *thought*.

Ink-horn

a classical flood (16th century)

About two-thirds of all the new words that arrived in English during the 16th century came from Latin. And Latin continued to supply words at a great rate during the 17th century too. It was all part of a mood to 'improve' the language. Many authors felt that they should use a lot of Latin words because, as the playwright Ben Jonson put it, 'Words borrowed of Antiquity do lend a kind of Majesty to style'.

But several writers overdid it. The English diplomat Thomas Wilson wrote a book on rhetoric in 1553 in which he quotes the kind of ornately obscure style that he saw emerging at the time. His example is of a letter written by a Lincolnshire gentleman wanting help in obtaining a job. I've modernised the spelling, but several of the words still need a gloss in order to be understood:

> Pondering, expending ['weighing'], and revoluting ['revolving'] with myself your ingent ['enormous'] affability, and ingenious capacity, for mundane affairs, I cannot but celebrate and extol your magnifical dexterity above all other.

Wilson roundly condemns this kind of writing. He

calls it 'outlandish English'. These people have forgotten their mother tongue, he says, and he goes on to remark that if their mothers were still alive they wouldn't be able to understand a word of what their children were saying.

The critics found a vivid way of describing this style: *ink-horn*, or *ink-pot*. An ink-horn, as its name suggests, was a small vessel, originally made of horn, for holding writing-ink. The Latin-derived words were scornfully called *ink-horn terms*. The idea was that these words were so lengthy that it would take a huge amount of ink to write them. People who used them a lot were said to 'smell of the ink-horn'.

The argument went backwards and forwards throughout the 16th century. Some found the classical words appealing; others argued for the superiority of ancient Anglo-Saxon words, which were felt to be short and clear. The scholar Sir John Cheke was quite certain about it. He writes in 1557: 'I am of the opinion that our tongue should be written clean and pure, unmixed and unmangled with borrowing of other tongues.'

The arguments about the use of classical vs Anglo-Saxon vocabulary resound across the centuries, and are still with us today (§74). In the 20th century, George Orwell was one who launched an attack on what he called 'pretentious diction' in a famous essay called 'Politics and the English Language'. But in the end it all comes down to balance. It's actually impossible to write English without using some words taken from other languages. Even Cheke, in his comment, has four of them: *opinion, mix, mangle* and *pure*. And both of Orwell's critical words come from Latin via French.

English vocabulary, in fact, shows Latin and Greek loanwords of different levels of difficulty. Some of the words that arrived in the 16th century and became a permanent part of English remain 'hard words' – *inveterate* and *susceptible*, for instance. But others are so much a part of modern daily expression that most people wouldn't realise they had classical origins, such as *benefit, climax, critic, explain, immediate, official* and *temperature*. Indeed, some, such as *fact, crisis* and *chaos*, would take up hardly any ink at all.

Dialect
regional variation (16th century)

The many manuscripts written in Old and Middle English show lots of evidence of regional variation, so it's a bit surprising that the word *dialect* doesn't actually appear in the language until the 16th century. But it doesn't take long thereafter for it to be widely used. And as awareness of local dialects increased, so did the collections of dialect words.

Spare a thought for the words that never get into dictionaries. Everyone knows that, in the part of the country where they live, there are local words and expressions which differ from those used further afield. But, precisely because they are local, they don't get into the big dictionaries. Dictionaries usually focus on the words in common educated use – the standard language. Only occasionally does a compiler allow in some local expressions. Dr Johnson was one who did. We find a few Scottish words in his dictionary, such as *mow* ('wry mouth') and *sponk* ('touchwood'), as well as some words from Staffordshire, such as *proud taylor* ('goldfinch') and *shaw* ('small wood'). Why these places? Five of his assistants were from Scotland, and Johnson himself was from Lichfield. Small nods of appreciation, perhaps.

Most dialect words remain uncelebrated until enthusiasts decide to collect and publish them. Once they do, we soon get a sense of just how numerous they are, and how important they are as a strand in the history of a language. One of the first serious attempts to locate dialect words in Britain was John Ray's *A Collection of English Words*, published in 1674. Ray is best known as 'the father of English natural history' because of his pioneering work in classifying plants and animals, but he was also a keen amateur linguist. Everywhere he travelled he made notes about the words he heard. He found *boor* in Cumberland, meaning 'parlour'; *bragget* in Lancashire and Cheshire, meaning 'spiced drink'; and *bourd* in Scotland, meaning 'jest'. His book contains hundreds of examples.

The greatest dialect wordsmith was Joseph Wright, born in 1855, son of a Yorkshire labourer.

He had no formal schooling, and he learned to read and write only when he was fifteen, but he went on to become professor of comparative philology at Oxford. He collected around half a million observations and between 1898 and 1905 published six large volumes as the *English Dialect Dictionary*. This is where to go if we want to find out how dialect words were used in the 18th and 19th centuries. Which counties used *agoggle* to mean 'trembling'? Berkshire and Hampshire. Where was *alkitotle* used to mean 'foolish fellow'? North Devon. In Wright's pages we see old linguistic worlds passing before our eyes.

But not always passing out of use. If we move on seventy years to a modern dialect survey, the *Linguistic Atlas of England* (1978), we find a surprising number of words still in use. Take *boosy*, the word for a 'cattle trough' or 'manger'. Wright found it chiefly used in the West Midlands, in an area running north–south between Cheshire and Herefordshire. It was still being used there in the 1960s. And in the 1990s, when the Survey of English Dialects published a dictionary, it was still there. The word turns up in John Ray's book too, and we find it again in the Anglo-Saxon gospels. Some dialect words have a very long life.

Bodgery

word-coiners (16th century)

The history of English contains thousands of words that never made it – coinages invented by individual writers that simply didn't catch on. There is just a single instance of *bodgery* recorded in the *Oxford English Dictionary*. It is from the playwright Thomas Nashe, who used it in 1599. It means 'bungling, botched work'.

Some 16th-century poets and playwrights seem almost to have coined words for a living. Nashe was second only to Shakespeare in the number of words whose first recorded use is found in his writing – nearly 800 – and several did become a permanent part of the language, such as *conundrum, grandiloquent, multifarious* and *balderdash*. Nashe also coined a word which would one day receive new life in science fiction: *earthling*.

But, like Shakespeare, quite a few of his coinages evidently didn't appeal. Either they were never used by anyone else, as far as we know, or they had a brief flurry of usage before being quietly dropped. Probably no tears would ever be shed over the loss of *collachrymate* ('accompanied by weeping') or *baggagery* ('worthless rabble'). But I rather regret that *bodgery* disappeared (though *bodge* and *bodger* are still heard in some dialects), along with *tongueman* ('good speaker') and *chatmate* ('gossip').

The list of words that never made it has a surreal

quality. From Philip Sidney we have *disinvite, hangworthy, rageful* and *triflingness*. From Edmund Spenser, *disadventurous, jolliment, schoolery* and *adviceful*. From John Marston, *cockall* ('perfection'), *bespirtle* ('to spot with vice'), *fubbery* ('cheating') and *glibbery* ('slippery') – creations Lewis Carroll would have been proud of. Sometimes it's impossible to say why one word stayed and another didn't. Why did Spenser's *tuneful* catch on but his *gazeful* did not?

However, you can never tell what will happen. *Musicry* was coined by John Marston, and nobody used it after him – until 1961, when a writer revived it for a book on the arts. Nashe's *chatmate* is currently the only instance of its use in the *Oxford English Dictionary*. But that will soon change, for in the world of chatrooms, social networking and internet dating, what do we find? Chatmates. There's hope for *bodgery* yet.

44 *Undeaf*
a word from Shakespeare (16th century)

In Shakespeare's *Richard II*, there's a scene in which Richard's uncle, John of Gaunt, expresses the hope that the king will listen to his dying words of advice about ruling more wisely. He wouldn't listen to me while I was alive, he says, but 'My death's sad tale may yet undeaf his ear' (II.i.16).

Undeaf. It's one of those words which must be a

genuine Shakespearean coinage. There are over 2,000 words in Shakespeare where the *Oxford English Dictionary* says he is the first recorded user. That doesn't mean to say he invented all of them. In many cases, he just happened to be the first person we know of to write an already existing word down on a page. The English of his time used an oath *God's blood* – usually shortened to *'sblood*. The first recorded use is in the first part of *Henry IV*. But people would have been swearing like that for years.

Undeaf is different. The man and woman in the street wouldn't have said that. Nor would they since. It's a vivid way of expressing the idea that Richard needs to listen. Shakespeare could have written 'My death's sad tale may open yet his ear'. *Undeaf* has more dramatic impact. Why? Because it's impossible. If you're deaf, you can't suddenly become undeaf. Deep down, John of Gaunt knows that there's nothing he can say that will change the king's behaviour.

Now if this were an isolated case, it wouldn't deserve a chapter in a wordbook. But it's by no means alone. Shakespeare loves to play with language in this way. He often takes a word and reverses its meaning by adding a prefix like *un-*, even if the action is strictly speaking impossible. In *Macbeth*, Lady Macbeth calls on the spirits to *unsex* her. Later in the same play, Malcolm affirms he is going to *unspeak* what he has said. In *Coriolanus*, the people are asked to *unshout* their earlier shouting.

If we go counting, we'll find 314 instances in the *Oxford English Dictionary* where Shakespeare is the first citation for an *un-* usage. Most of them are adjectives, such as *uncomfortable* and *uneducated*, but there are no fewer than sixty-two cases where the prefix has been added to an already existing verb. Some of them, such as *unlock*, *untie* and *unbend*, have become a routine part of the language. But *undeaf* and several others have not.

What Shakespeare does today, the rest of the world does tomorrow. And indeed, it has become a routine feature of creative English expression to make new words by adding a prefix such as *un-*. The language seems to be returning to its Germanic roots, for coinages with *un-* were very common in Old English, and words like *unfriend* (§**36**, **99**) have their parallels in *unwine* ('enemy', literally *un* + *wine*, pronounced 'wee-nuh', 'friend'). In recent times we have had hundreds of coinages, such as *uncool*, *unfunny*, *ungimmicky*, *unsorry*, *untouristy*, *untrendy*, *un-with-it* and *unyoung*. Unyoung? 'Why not just say old?' you might ask. But there's a difference. Many senior citizens refuse to accept that they are old, though they might reluctantly agree that they are unyoung.

Skunk

an early Americanism (17th century)

In 1585, Thomas Hariot travelled with Sir Walter Raleigh in his attempt to establish a colony on Roanoke Island in Virginia. When he returned to England, he wrote *A Briefe and True Report of the New Found Land of Virginia*, in which he gives a great deal of information about the place and the people. He identifies 'two kinds of small beasts greater than conies [rabbits] which are very good meat', naming them *saquenúckot* and *maquówoc*.

People have puzzled over which animals these must have been. Were they raccoons, opossums, muskrats ... or even skunks? The first clear use of the name *skunk* doesn't turn up until 1634, in another account of early America. The *Oxford English Dictionary* derives it from a different Indian language from the one spoken in Roanoke. But *saquenúckot* certainly looks as if it might be the origin of *skunk*.

Skunk is an early Americanism. It was one of dozens of words that were borrowed from the Algonquian languages in the early 1600s. Many of them didn't last. Nobody today (except possibly in some dialects) talks about a *sagamore* ('chief') or a *pocosin* ('swamp'). But several words did survive, such as *caribou, moccasin, moose, opossum, persimmon, powwow, tomahawk, totem* and *wigwam*. Today there are hundreds of words that distinguish American from British English (§58).

It's sometimes difficult to recognise Indian words in early writings. The indigenous languages were very different from anything Europeans had encountered before, and they had no idea how to spell the words they heard. Captain John Smith arrived in Virginia in 1606 and explored the new territory at length, writing an account of the meetings between the colonists and the local tribes. He's best known for the famous story of his escape from execution by the Indian chief Powhatan through the intervention of Powhatan's daughter, Pocahontas. He sent an account of the colony back to England, where it was published in 1608.

His book contains many Amerindian place-names, and at one point – during a visit to the Powhatan Indians – a new noun:

> Arriving at Weramocomoco, their Emperour
> proudly lying uppon a Bedstead a foote high, upon
> tenne or twelves Mattes, richly hung with Manie
> Chaynes of great Pearles about his necke, and
> covered with a great Covering of Rahaughcums.

Rahaughcums? A little later in his book he spells it *Raugroughcuns*. These are the first brave attempts to write down *raccoons* in English.

Shibboleth
a word from King James (17th century)

The King James Bible, published in 1611, is often called the 'Authorised Version' of the Bible because – as it says on its title-page – it was 'appointed to be read in churches'. Earlier translations of the Bible, such as William Tyndale's (§37), had introduced many new words and idioms into English, but the King James Bible popularised them in a way that hadn't been possible before.

The team of translators didn't actually introduce many new words and phrases themselves. They say in their Preface that their job was not to make a new translation, but rather 'to make a good one better'. They had no choice in the matter, actually, as they'd been given guidelines, approved by King James, which required them to use a previous edition (known as the Bishops' Bible) as their model. As a result, there are very few words and phrases which actually originate in the text of the King James Bible.

Only forty-three words are currently listed in the *Oxford English Dictionary* as having a first recorded use there. They include several religion-specific expressions, such as *Galilean* (as a noun) and *rose of Sharon*, as well as a few general words, such as *battering-ram, escaper* and *rosebud*. Far more important are the idioms which the Bible popularised: there are over 250, such as *salt of the earth, a thorn in the flesh, root and branch, out of the mouths of babes* and *how are the mighty fallen*. Their significance in the shaping of English mustn't be forgotten. Idioms are part of vocabulary too.

Shibboleth is not among the forty-three, because this word had been used in all the earlier English translations. But there is nonetheless something distinctive about the way it appears in the King James Bible: its spelling. *Shibboleth* appears in the Old Testament Book of Judges. We are told how the regional accent of an unfortunate Ephraimite, who had fallen into the hands of the Gileadites, reveals his origins:

> Then said they unto him, Say now Shibboleth:
> and he said Sibboleth: for he could not frame to
> pronounce it right. Then they took him, and slew
> him at the passages of Jordan.

The spelling of the word varies in the earlier translations. In John Wycliffe's version, the Ephraimite seems to have more of a lisp, for he says *Thebolech* instead of *Sebolech*. Other versions have *Schibboleth* and *Scibboleth*. The Geneva Bible and the King James Bible both have *Shibboleth*, and it is this spelling which has prevailed.

But even biblical words and phrases don't stand still, and in later centuries *shibboleth* developed several new senses – a custom, a habit, a catchword, a moral formula, an imaginary error, an unfounded belief. There are lots of shibboleths in the study of language. Some people think it's wrong to end a sentence with a preposition (*That's the man I spoke to*) or to split an infinitive (*to boldly go*) or to pronounce *H* as 'haitch', even though such forms are widely found in modern English. These are the kinds of issue, often called *linguistic shibboleths*, that have fuelled usage debates since the 18th century. They are debates in which emotions sometimes run high – though never, as far as I know, having an outcome like that of the biblical precedent.

47 *Bloody*

an emerging swear-word (17th century)

On 11 April 1914, the *Daily Sketch*, a London tabloid newspaper, ran this headline:

> TO-NIGHT'S 'PYGMALION', IN WHICH MRS
> PATRICK CAMPBELL IS EXPECTED TO CAUSE
> THE GREATEST THEATRICAL SENSATION FOR
> YEARS.

What was all the fuss about? George Bernard Shaw had given Mrs Campbell, in the character of Eliza Doolittle, a dangerous line to say: 'Not bloody likely.' Nobody had said such a swear-word on a public stage before. The paper went on:

> Mr. Shaw Introduces a Forbidden Word.
> WILL 'MRS PAT' SPEAK IT?

She did. And the audience loved it. There was a gasp of surprise, then everyone roared with laughter.

It had taken *bloody* a thousand years to cause such a stir. It was first used by the Anglo-Saxons with such meanings as 'bleeding' and 'stained with blood', and it developed a range of related senses to do with slaughter and bloodshed. It's a point we have to watch when we listen to Shakespeare. When Macbeth tells us that his 'bloody cousins' have fled from Scotland (*Macbeth* III.i.29), he isn't swearing but accusing them of a murderous stabbing.

The word began to be used in an emphatic way towards the end of the 17th century – meaning 'very', but with an intensifying force. When Jonathan Swift, writing a letter to Stella in 1711, talks about the day being *bloody hot*, he means 'very hot indeed'. There's no hint of any impropriety. The word seems to have been used in colloquial speech by all kinds of people at that time.

But during the 18th century the sensitive ears of the aristocratic and respectable classes turned against *bloody*, probably because of its associations with rowdiness and rough behaviour. Aristocratic rowdies were known as *bloods*, so to be *bloody drunk* was to be 'drunk as a blood'. (We have the same association today, when we say 'drunk as a lord'.) The historical association with blood and mayhem would have appealed to those for whom rough behaviour was a way of life, and this reinforced upper- and middle-class antipathy. By the middle of the 18th century it was definitely a 'bad word'. Dr Johnson described it in his *Dictionary* of 1755 as 'very vulgar'. That settled it.

People who wanted to be emphatic had to find socially more acceptable alternatives. *Deuced, rattling* and *ripping* became popular. *Bleeding* was used first by Cockneys in the 1850s, but – perhaps for that very reason – never acquired upper-class respectability. *Blooming*, used from the 1880s, was more success-ful. *Ruddy*, slightly less so. Dozens of words became fashionable, such as *devilish, damned, jolly, awfully* and *terribly*.

It was all a very British thing. Americans have never understood the British timidity towards using *bloody*, and Australians find it even more puzzling. In both Australia and the USA, the word is used as an intensifer, yet without the aura of rudeness which is part of its historical baggage in the UK.

Usage in Britain is slowly adapting to the world scene – though very slowly. *Bloody* is no longer printed as *b----y*, and it isn't one of the words relegated to late-night television viewing. But the sensitivity is still there. In 2006 a television ad for Tourism Aus-tralia included the sentence 'So where the bloody hell are you?' This was too much for the regulators at the British Advertising Clearance Centre, who cut it out, and restored it (for late-evening viewing) only after a huge row. So I'm not expecting to hear a BBC weather forecaster say in the foreseeable future: 'It's been bloody hot today ...'

Lakh

a word from India (17th century)

Here are two recent newspaper headlines from India.

Nearly 5 lakh foreigners throng India for cheap treatment

Rs 50-lakh divorce for runaway wife

Lakh. A Hindi word meaning 100,000. So, *5 lakh* is half a million. *50 lakh* (Rs = rupees) is 5 million. It's one of the words you need to know. The figures get bigger when you turn to the business pages. There you find people talking about *crores* as well. A *crore* is 10 million.

These words arrived in English in the early 1600s. Already several Indian words had entered the language from earlier contacts. A *godown* is a place where goods are stored – a warehouse. It's recorded in a voyager's report of 1588. It comes from a Malay word, *godong,* and probably took its English form because people heard it as 'go down' – the storehouses were often in cellars.

Once the British East India Company was established (in 1600), travel to and from the region greatly increased. It wasn't long before the local languages began to provide English with new words, and several eventually lost their cultural associations with India. From the north of the Indian subcontinent, where Indo-European languages such as Hindi were spoken, we find such 17th-century words as *bungalow, dungaree, guru, juggernaut, punch* (the drink) and *pundit*. Examples from the south, where Dravidian languages such as Tamil were spoken, were *atoll, catamaran, cheroot, pariah, teak* and *curry*. In the Far East, Tibetan, Malay, Chinese, Japanese and other languages all began to supply new words, such as *ginseng, bamboo, ketchup, kimono, junk* (the ship) and *chaa* – this last one not immediately recognisable in that form, but the origin of *tea* (and, of course, colloquial *char*).

The various routes to India also brought English into renewed contact with languages such as Arabic, Turkish and Persian. Quite a few Arabic words, for example, had come into Middle English, especially introducing scientific notions such as *alchemy* and *almanac*, but in the 16th and 17th centuries there is a significant expansion. In many cases, the Arabic words entered English through another language: *assassin*, for example, is ultimately from Arabic *hash-shashin* ('hashish-eaters'), but came to English via Italian *assassino*.

The new words reflect local life and customs. Arabic loans include *fakir, harem, jar, magazine, sherbet, minaret, alcove* and *sofa*. From Turkish we find *vizier, horde, kiosk, coffee* and *yoghurt*. From Persian, *bazaar, caravan, divan, shah* and *turban*. From Hebrew, *sanhedrin, shekel, shibboleth, torah* and *hallelujah*.

Today, the regional English vocabulary of a country like India is extensive indeed, and continues to develop. The 20th century has seen a host of food words such as *tandoori, samosa* and *pakora.* Among the colloquial words to arrive have been *cushy, doolally* and *loot* ('money'). A new lease of computational life has been given to *avatar.* And in Indian newspapers of the 2000s we will find such local forms as *speed-money* ('bribe'), *timepass* ('way of passing the time'), *timewaste* ('time-wasting') and *petrol bunk* ('petrol station'), as well as new uses of older forms, such as *hi-fi* ('fancy', as in *hi-fi clothes*). Even the basic vocabulary of the language can be affected, such as kinship terms. Who is your *co-brother*? The man who married your wife's sister. And your *cousin-sister*? Your female first cousin.

49 *Fopdoodle*

a lost word (17th century)

People started to use the word *fopdoodle* in the 17th century. It was a combination of *fop* and *doodle,* two words very similar in meaning. A *fop* was a fool. A *doodle* was a simpleton. So a *fopdoodle* was a fool twice over. Country bumpkins would be called fopdoodles. But so could the fashionable set, because *fop* had also developed the meaning of 'vain dandy'. Dr Johnson didn't like them at all. In his *Dictionary* he defines *fopdoodle* as 'a fool, an insignificant wretch'.

Fopdoodle is one of those words that people regret are lost when they hear about them. There are several delightful items in Johnson's *Dictionary* which we no longer use. He tells us that *nappiness* was 'the quality of having a nap'. A *bedswerver* was 'one that is false to the bed'. A *smellfeast* was 'a parasite, one who haunts good tables'. A *worldling* was 'a mortal set upon profits'. A *curtain-lecture* was 'a reproof given by a wife to her husband in bed'.

Every generation gives us new words which eventually disappear. I once did a study of words that were being fêted as 'new' in the 1960s. Over half of them have gone out of everyday use now. Do you recall *Rachmanism, Powellism, peaceniks, dancercise, frugs* and *flower people*? All frequent in the 1960s. Historical memories today.

It's always been like this. But dictionaries are notoriously reluctant to leave words out – for the obvious reason that it's very difficult to say when a word actually goes out of use. You can spot a new word easily; but how do you know that an old word has finally died? Did *grody* (slang 'nasty, dirty') die out in the 1970s, or is it still being used in the back streets of Boston?

On the whole, dictionaries keep words in, either until constraints of space force some pruning, or a new editorial broom looks at the word-list afresh and says 'Enough is enough'. That's presumably what happened in 2008, when the editors of the Collins dictionary decided that some words are so rare these days that nobody would ever want to look them up. They blamed pressure on space in the dictionary:

A group of US scholars offer a toast to Samuel Johnson, on the occasion
the 200th anniversary of the publication of his Dictionary *in 1955. A*
nson Society was founded in 1910, based in his home town of Lichfield,
ere the Birthplace Museum has a permanent exhibition of his life and
es.

with 2,000 new words to include, several old words would, regrettably, have to go. They included *abstergent* ('cleansing or scouring'), *compossible* ('possible in coexistence with something else'), *fatidical* ('prophetic'), *fubsy* ('short and stout'), *niddering* ('cowardly') and *skirr* ('a whirring or grating sound, as of the wings of birds in flight').

The Times was having none of this. In its issue of 22 September 2008 it launched a campaign: 'How you can help to save some cherished words from oblivion.' People could vote to save the words they fancied. Collins, which is owned by News Corporation, the parent company of *The Times*, agreed that words would be granted a reprieve if evidence of their popularity emerged.

It was a curious headline, if you think about it, for if these words were being genuinely cherished, why should they be in this list at all? Nevertheless, there was quite a reaction. Andrew Motion went on record as supporting *skirr*. Stephen Fry was all for saving *fubsy*. Indeed, a 'save fubsy' online petition group was set up.

Just because words are left out of a dictionary of standard English doesn't mean that they have disappeared from the language, of course. Some of the words remain alive and well in regional dialects. I know *niddering* and *skirr* are still used in parts of Scotland and the north of England, and *fubsy* (along with *fub*, 'stout') is mentioned in several dialect books.

It's a daring decision, to leave a word out, because

you can never predict the future with language. A word or phrase can be obsolescent, then suddenly have its fortunes reversed by being used by some celebrity. Or attitudes change towards a word, so that one generation loves it and the next hates it and the next loves it again. But whatever has happened to words in the past, the future is going to be very different. The internet is changing everything, because in an electronic world dictionaries can be of unlimited size, pages are time-stamped and nothing disappears (§83). The internet is already the largest corpus of attested historical language data we have ever known. In that dictionary words never die. Even *fopdoodle*, attracting a lowly 8,000 hits on Google in 2011, will live on. If words could talk, they would say they had finally achieved what they always wanted: immortality.

Billion

a confusing ambiguity (17th century)

As scientists extended the boundaries of knowledge, so they needed larger numerals to talk about what they found. A million, known since the Middle Ages, wasn't enough. They needed billions, trillions and more. Popular usage followed suit. People were already saying things like *a million to one* and *one in a million* in the 17th century. Then inflation set in. *One in a billion* sounded much more impressive.

But what did *billion* mean, exactly? The English

thought of the six zeros in a million (1,000,000) as being a functional unit, so the next value up was going to be twice six zeros (1,000,000,000,000). *Billion* in Britain thus meant 'a million millions' – a 'long-scale system', as it later came to be called. But French mathematicians later went in a different direction. They thought of 1,000,000 as two groups of three zeros, so for them the next unit up was three groups of three zeros – that is, 1,000,000,000. In France, *billion* thus meant 'a thousand million' – a 'short-scale system'.

The history of usage is complicated and varies enormously from country to country. Britain stayed with the long-scale system, but in the 19th century the USA adopted the short-scale system. For over a century, American English dictionaries recommended 'thousand million' and British dictionaries 'million million'. Then, in 1974, Britain capitulated. The prime minister of the time, Harold Wilson, made a statement to the House of Commons:

> The word 'billion' is now used internationally to mean 1,000 million and it would be confusing if British Ministers were to use it in any other sense.

However, usage doesn't take kindly to government statements. Although officially a billion is now a thousand million in the UK, people are still aware of the older use, and uncertainty is common. So whenever I use *billion*, I gloss it. If I say that 'English is spoken by 2 billion people', I immediately add, '2 thousand million', to be on the safe side.

It's the normal state of affairs in a language for everyday words to have more than one sense. We only have to look in a dictionary to see that. There's usually no ambiguity, because when we use the words in sentences we see which sense is involved. On its own, *bed* is ambiguous: it could mean (for example) a place where we sleep or a place where we plant flowers. But we have no problem interpreting *I stayed in bed until ten* or *Look at that lovely bed of roses*.

It's unusual to find a scientific term developing an ambiguity of the kind displayed by *billion*. Normally, when scientists create terms, they're accepted by the whole scientific community. There are standard definitions of such words as *hydrogen*, *atom* and *pterodactyl*, and we don't expect to find differences between American and British usage. But here's a mathematical term which is not only ambiguous but where the ambiguity doesn't disappear when we put it in a sentence. When we read, 'The disaster has lost the company a billion pounds', we can't tell how much has been lost. *Billion* reminds us of the ever-present dangers of ambiguity in the history of the language.

Of course, for most of us, the difference isn't important. It's simply 'a lot'. And the language has come to reflect this 'couldn't care less' attitude. The *-illion* ending is now used to express very large but indefinite amounts. In the mid-20th century we find *zillion* and *bazillion*, later *gazillion* and *kazillion*. People with really huge amounts of money were *zillionaires*. *The Record*, a New Jersey newspaper, took the coinages to new heights when it talked about an economic crisis in 1990:

> The savings-and-loan industry bailout, which as of yesterday was expected to cost taxpayers $752.6 trillion skillion, is now expected to cost $964.3 hillion jillion bazillion, not including the Christmas party.

Doubtless these words got a new lease of life during the banking crisis twenty years later.

 ## Yogurt
a choice of spelling (17th century)

How do you spell *yogurt*? When the word arrived in English from Turkish in the early 17th century, people made several stabs at it. The first recorded usage is *yoghurd*. Then we get *yogourt*. Then *yahourt, yaghourt, yogurd, yoghourt, yooghort, yughard, yughurt* and *yohourth*. In the 19th century, there was a trend to simplify, and *yogurt* emerged as the front runner. It still is. In 2011 it was getting some 14 million hits on Google, with *yoghurt* 8 million and everything else a long way behind.

Preferences vary somewhat between countries, however. *Yogurt* is the norm in the USA. In the UK, both are used, but *yoghurt* is three times more common than *yogurt*. *Yogourt* has achieved some presence in Canada, because of its French-looking character, but even there *yogurt* is more widespread. In Australia and New Zealand, *yoghurt* is commoner than *yogurt*, but *yogurt* is catching up, probably because of exposure to American and internet usage. *Yogurt* is catching up in the UK too. You have to be careful where you look, when you consult a dictionary. Some give *yogurt* as the headword, which places it after *yogi* and *yogic*. Others give *yoghurt* as the headword, which places it before.

Yogurt is not the only word that turns up at different places in a dictionary depending on how it's spelled. The differences between British and American spelling can lead to very different locations. Depending on the dictionary you use, you'll look under either MO- or MU- for *moustache/mustache*, under PY- or PA- for *pyjamas/pajamas* and under FO- or FE- for *foetus/ fetus*. The problem is especially noticeable when the first letters of a word are affected. At least *aeroplane* and *airplane* keep you in letter A, and *tyre* and *tire* in T. But we have to make some big jumps with *oestrogen* and *estrogen*, *aesthetics* and *esthetics* and *kerb* and *curb*. A good dictionary will always anticipate the problem and include a cross-reference to get you from one place to the other.

Probably the commercial use of the word will condition the ultimate success of one *yogurt* spelling over the others. If you explore the yogurt-making world, you'll encounter a whole family of derived forms. There are compound words such as *yogurt machine*, *yogurt maker* and *yogurt freezer*. Adjectives such as *yogurt-like*, *yogurtish* and *yogurty*. And brave new worlds too, it seems, judging by the name of an American international chain of frozen yogurt stores – *Yogurtland*.

Gazette

a taste of journalese (17th century)

The year 1665 is known for the Great Plague. Charles II moved his court out of London to Oxford. But how would the court keep in touch with the news? Publisher Henry Muddiman was authorised to produce what is often called 'the first English newspaper', the *Oxford Gazette*. When the danger was over, and the court moved back to London, the paper changed its name, becoming the *London Gazette* in February 1666.

The word *gazette* had come over from the continent, where it was used to describe a popular – though by all accounts not very reliable – news-sheet. One commentator described gazettes as including 'idle intelligences and flim flam tales' – frivolous nonsense. Perhaps for that reason, it was soon displaced in everyday usage by the word *newspaper*, whose first recorded use is in 1667, written as two words: *news paper*. However, *gazette* remained as the name of various official journals. If you were *gazetted*, you were the subject of an official announcement. And the journalists who wrote for them were called *gazetteers*.

The Oxford Gazette.

Publiſhed by Authority.

Oxon, Nov. 7.

THis day the Reverend Dr. *Walter Blandford*, Warden of *Wadham Colledge* in this Univerſity, was Elected Lord Biſhop of this See, vacant by the death of Dr. *Paul*, late Biſhop here.

Oxon, Nov. 12. This day His Majeſty in Council, according to the uſual cuſtom, having the Roll of Sheriffs preſented to him, pricked theſe perſons following, to be Sheriffs for the ſucceeding year, in their reſpective Counties of *England* and *Wales.*

Berks.	Baſil Brent, *Eſquire.*
Bedford.	Tho. Snagge, *Eſq;*
Buckingham	Simon Bennet, *Eſq;*
Cumberland.	Sir William Dalſton, *Baronet.*
Cheſter.	Sir John Arderne, *Knight.*
Cambridge.	Sir Tho. Willis, *Kt.* and *Baronet.*
Cornwal.	Tho. Dorrel, *Eſq;*
Devon.	John Kelland, *Eſq;*
Dorſet.	Roger Clavel, *Eſq;*
Derby.	Sir Samuel Sleigh, *Knight.*
Yorkſhire.	Sir Francis Cobb, *Knight.*
Eſſex.	Sir Heneage Fetherſtone, *Baronet.*
Gloceſter.	Sir Richard Cox, *Baronet.*
Hertford.	Sir Jonathan Keat, *Baronet.*
Hereford.	Tho. Rod, *Eſq;*
Kent.	Sir Humphrey Miller, *Baronet.*
Lancaſter.	William Spencer *Eſq;*
Leiceſter.	Sir Edward Smith, *Baronet.*
Lincolne.	Sir John Brownlow *Kt.* and *Baronet.*
Monmouth.	Walter Morgan of Landillo Patholly, *Eſq;*
Northumberland.	William Middleton, *Eſq;*
Northampton.	Joſeph Hanbury *Eſq;*
Norfolk.	Sir John Hobard. *Baronet.*
Nottingham.	John White of Congrave, *Eſq;*
Oxford.	Tho. Wheate of Glimſton, *Eſq;*
Rutland.	Charles Halford *Eſq;*
Shropſhire.	Sir Humph. Briggs.
Somerſet.	Sir Hugh Smith, *Baronet.*
Stafford.	Fran. Laweſon, *alias* Fowler *Eſq;*
Suffolk.	Sir Edmund Bacon, *Baronet.*
Southampton.	Tho. Neal, *Eſq;*
Surry.	Sir John Evelyn, *Baronet.*
Suſſex.	Robert Fowle, *Eſq;*
Warwick.	Charles Bentley, *Eſq;*
Worceſter.	Sir William Cooks of Norgrave *Kt.*
Wilts.	Sir John Weld, *Kt.*
Angleſey.	Rowland Bulkley, *Eſq;*
Brecknock.	Hugh Powel, *Eſq;*
Cardigan.	James Stedman, *Eſq;*
Caernarvan.	Tho. Maderne, *Eſq;*
Denbigh.	Sir Charles Goodman.
Flint.	Sir Roger Molyn.
Glamorgan.	WilliamBaſſat of Benbeſkin, *Eſq;*
Merioneth.	Lewis Lloyd, *Eſq;*
Montgomery.	Ed. Kynaſton. *Eſq;*
Pembroke.	Sir Herbert Perrot.
Radnor.	Nich. Taylor, *Eſq;*
Carmarthen.	William Lloyd, *Eſq;*

Paris, Nov. 14. Monſieur *de Turenne* is not yet returned, but expected here every day. Moſt of the Gentry of *Nivernois* & *Bourgne* are ſaid to have withdrawn themſelves, and got into a place of ſtrength: one Monſieur *de Cannillac* having been put to death by the Commiſſioners of the *Grands Jours* : It ſeems they have laid ſome new Taxes or Impoſitions on thoſe parts, There are Troups marching againſt them, and it is thought they will ſoon be reduced. my Lord *Aubigny* Lord Almoner to her Majeſty, having lain ſick ſome time here of an Hydropſie attended with a Flux, is this week dead.

Paris, Nov. 18. The Mareſchal *de Turenne* arrived here on Sunday laſt from the Frontiers, whence he brings account that the Succors intended againſt the Prince of *Munſter* had paſſed in ſmall parties, and that they had been received at *Maſtricht* by Monſieur *Beverning* in the name of the States General.

Guernzey, Octob. 30. Yeſterday came in our Road the *Unity* Frigat, Captain *Paſſard* Commander, who brought in a Prize Captain *John Gilſon* of *Flaſhing* being a Privateer of 7 Guns, and 45 Men.

Chatham, Nov. 4. Captain *Eliot* Commander of the *Saphire*, has taken 3 Buſſes, two of them out of 50 at the *Dogger-ſands*, under the Protection of four of their Men of War. In hispaſſage home, tis ſaid, he ſaw ſeveral tops of Ships, Maſts, &c. which ſeemed to be the effects of ſome Wreck, which God he thanked we cannot hearto have been any of the Engliſh Ships.

Oxon, Nov. 12. Not knowing what account the Publick has hitherto received of the progreſs of the Prince of *Munſter's* Arms, we have thought it not improper without further repetition, to give an accouct of ſuch places as he at preſent ſtands poſſeſt of in the enemies Country, *viz.* The Caſtle and Territory of *Lorin* (being of right his own, and for many yearsunjuſtly detained from him) the Caſtle of *Litchtenwarde* and the Towns of *Lochem, Dotechem, Dieperheim, Goer, Enſcheide, Olde ſel, Orthmueſchen, ardenborg. Onnuan, Vin, Wildenborg, Keppel Almelve, Hingle, Granenborg,* and *Vennebrog* and now more lately *Winſchot,* with the Fort of *Brugge en Jeante,* the Caſtle of *Wedde,* and the Cloyſter of *Appel,* out of which a party of his had ſome time before been forced by the *Hollanders.* And it is confirmed to us by ſeveral good hands from *Bruſſels,* that he has taken the ſtrong Fort of *Beartange,* and *Reid,* a Sea-port, ſituated near *Dromme* and *Delfſi- Iſle,* in divers of which places his Highneſs has left very conſiderable Garriſons, beſides his Field Army, which conſiſts of 18000 Foot, and 6000 Horſe effective.

Deal, Nov. 8. The Wind ſince my laſt continues very High, but I hear of no harm done yet. The *Phenix* hath brought in a Prize here.

Norwich, Nov. 8. I lately received from a good hand in *Rochel* dated *Octo. 28.* a ſhort account of the taking the Iſland S. *Uſtache,* which for the manner of the attempt, may not be unworthy the Communication ; it was brought by a French *Weſt-India* Ship, which came from S. *Chryſtophers* about 3 Leagues from it, and runs thus. That on the 12 of *Aug.* about 300 of the Forces belonging to *Jamaica* went thither with a reſolution of an attaque. There is but one landing place in the whole Iſland, & that of ſuch difficult acceſs, that but 2 at moſt can go abreaſt, and aſcent to an eminent place, in the top of which was a ſtrong Fort, which on this occaſion had been well furniſhed with Powder & Guns left by *de Ruyter,* & Man'd with 450 ſoldiers, who were neverthelesſ ſo ſurpriſed at the boldneſs of the undertaking, that they delivered themſelves up with very little reſiſtance.

Plimouth, Nov. 5. The weather of late hath been very

The early newspapers looked very different from those of today. Notably, they had no banner headlines running across the page. A news item in the *Oxford Gazette* began simply with its place of origin and the date, such as *Paris, Nov 18*. Banner headlines didn't become a feature of the daily press until the end of the 19th century.

Once they did, there was an immediate effect on language. The headline had to catch the eye and capture interest. With a very limited amount of space available, short words became privileged, and a new lexical style quickly evolved. We see it mainly in the tabloid press, but all newspapers are to some extent influenced by the need to keep headlines short and snappy.

So we are less likely to see headlines in which people *abolish, forbid, reduce, swindle* and *resign*. Rather, they will *axe, ban, cut, con* and *quit* (or simply *go*). We will rarely read of a *division of opinion*, an *encouraging sign*, an *argument* or an *agreement*. Instead, it will be a *rift, boost, row* or *deal*. And many short words are doubly appealing because they carry an extra emotional charge: *fury, clash, slam, soar* ...

All this is a long way from the cultivated and elaborate language of the *Oxford Gazette*, reporting events in the Anglo-Dutch War:

> Not knowing what account the Publick has
> hitherto received of the progress of the prince of
> Munster's Arms, we have thought it not improper
> without further repetition, to give an account of

such places as he at present stands possest of in the enemies Country ...

The writer goes on to list the various forts and ships that the prince had captured. How might a modern newspaper deal with such a situation? If past tabloid performance is anything to go by, it might even be a single word. Few headlines have stayed in the popular memory longer than the one that appeared in *The Sun* for 4 May 1982, reporting the attack on the Argentine cruiser *General Belgrano* in the Falklands War: GOTCHA (§88).

Tea

a social word (17th century)

On 25 September 1660, Samuel Pepys wrote in his *Diary*: 'I did send for a cup of tee (a China drink) of which I never had drunk before.' The beverage had been imported into Europe from China early in the 17th century, but the British seem not to have taken to it until mid-century. Pepys probably got his tea from one of the coffee houses which had begun to sell both liquid and dry tea in the 1650s. The first recorded reference to the word is 1655.

In 1661, tea-taking was introduced into the Restoration court by Queen Catherine, the Portuguese wife of Charles II. It immediately became a fashionable ritual, accompanied by an elegant apparatus of silver spoons, pots, stands, tongs and caddies, and an occasion for conversation. But the innovation was taken up by other levels of society too. As its price fell, everyone adopted the habit, upstairs and downstairs alike, taking tea usually twice a day.

The linguistic consequences were both functional and social. Over the next fifty years we find a family of words introduced to describe all the bits and pieces needed in order to drink tea efficiently, such as *tea-pot, tea-spoon, tea-water, tea-cup* (with handle, unlike in China), *tea-dish, tea-house* and *tea-room*. And a century later the family multiplied in size when society recognised the crucial notion of *tea-time* – the ideal midway point between midday and evening meals.

Thereafter, the technology becomes more sophisticated and the occasions more elaborate. Few words can have developed so many uses so quickly as *tea*. We find *tea-treats, tea-saucers, tea-trays* and *tea sets*. People bought from *tea-shops* and made *tea-visits*. In the 19th century, we find *tea-bags, tea-cakes, tea-towels* and *tea-services*. High society met for *tea circles* and *tea nights* and rang *tea-bells* for service. New fashions introduced *tea-gowns* and *tea-jackets*. In the 20th century, we find an extension into the world of business and manufacture, where *tea trolleys* and *tea wagons* are pushed by *tea ladies* and *tea girls*. People take *tea breaks* and visit *tea bars*. *Teashades* (wire-rimmed sunglasses) were popular among 1960s' rock-stars such as John Lennon and Ozzy Osbourne.

Meanwhile, the word was worming its way into 20th-century English idiom. *Not for all the tea in China* seems to have started in Australia. *Tea and sympathy* became popular following a stage play and film from the 1950s. The most curious idiomatic development was *cup of tea*. The expression was originally used for a person, as in *You're a nice strong cup of tea*. Then it became a focus of interest, either a person (*He's my cup of tea*) or a topic (*Science fiction is more my cup of tea*). We then find it used in a negative way (*Science fiction isn't my cup of tea*) and then as an expression of comparison (*That's a very different cup of tea*). Nobody knows how the idiom started. It feels like something that would come out of a Victorian music-hall, but its earliest recorded use in the *Oxford English Dictionary* isn't until 1908.

The story of *tea* isn't over yet. It continues to be reported in street slang in a huge range of expressions, though one never knows just how widely used they are. *To go tea tax?* To get really angry. *Tea-brained?* An obtuse person. In 2009, *tea* even became a political acronym in the USA, when the *Tea Party* was formed. *TEA?* Taxed Enough Already.

Disinterested

a confusible (17th century)

Interest is one of those words where you have to look carefully at the context to see what is meant. It started life in English in the 15th century as a legal expression. If you have *an interest in an estate*, you have a right or claim to some of it. Later it developed a financial sense. If you hold *an interest in a company*, you have a financial stake in it. More general senses emerged. When people say they *have our interests at heart*, they mean our good. When politicians say *It's in your interest to vote for me*, they mean our advantage. And in the 17th century we find the meaning which eventually became the most common modern use: a feeling of concern or curiosity about something. *What are your interests?*

Some of this ambiguity spilled over into the adjective, *interested*. The earliest recorded meaning is the curiosity one. *I'm interested* meant 'I'm curious to know'. But soon after, the self-seeking meaning arrived. *I'm interested* now meant 'I spy a personal advantage', and people began to talk of *interested parties* in a venture.

This leads us to the negative form. How did people express the idea that they were *not* interested? Two prefixes were the chief candidates: *un-* and *dis-*. Which should be used? There are dozens of cases in the 16th and 17th centuries of people experimenting with both. Should they say *discontent* or *uncontent*? *Discomfortable* or *uncomfortable*? Sometimes the *dis-* form survived (as in *discontent*). Sometimes the *un-* form did (as in *uncomfortable*). And in others, both forms survived with different meanings.

What makes *interested* so interesting is that

both forms survived, but with the meanings totally overlapping.

- *Disinterested* is first recorded in the early 17th century. It meant 'unconcerned, indifferent'. By the mid-century it had come to mean 'impartial, unbiased'.
- *Uninterested* is first recorded in the mid-17th century with the sense of 'impartial, unbiased'. A century later it developed the sense of 'unconcerned, indifferent'.

We might think this would be a recipe for semantic disaster. By 1750 each form could express the same two different meanings.

Dr Johnson tried to sort it out. In his *Dictionary* he gave *disinterested* the unbiased sense ('not influenced by private profit') and *uninterested* the 'incurious' sense ('not having interest'). From then on, people strove to maintain the distinction – but with only partial success. In the 20th century, surveys showed that over a quarter of all the uses of *disinterested* in Britain meant 'bored', and nearly twice as many used it in this sense in the USA. People regularly say such things as 'After a while I became disinterested in football, and stopped going to matches.'

As the 20th century progressed, such usages came to be roundly condemned by people who felt that an important distinction was being lost. In fact, the context makes it perfectly clear what is meant. The usage wouldn't have developed at all if there had been any real ambiguity. And it evidently wasn't a big issue in Henry Fowler's day, for he doesn't even mention it in his *Dictionary of Modern English Usage* in 1926. But concern evidently grew in the following decades, and when Sir Ernest Gowers came to revise Fowler in the 1960s he added an entry on *disinterested* and pleaded for the distinction to be rescued, 'if it is not too late'.

It wasn't. Today, the difference between the two words remains a live issue, thanks to its flagship status among usage pundits. But for many, the controversy has engendered a distrust. If they write *disinterested* meaning 'unbiased', will it be understood in the sense they intend? The feeling has grown that perhaps it would be better to avoid the word altogether, and use a synonym. The future of *disinterested* remains in the balance.

55 *Polite*
a matter of manners (17th century)

We learn to be linguistically polite at a very early age. It starts during the fourth year of life, when children have acquired enough language to have proper conversations. Parents start drilling. 'Say please.' 'Say sorry.' 'I haven't heard that little word yet.' 'Don't talk with your mouth full.' The kids learn that there are words that should not be used in polite company. These then become the most desirable words of all, of course!

As we grow up, we learn more sophisticated expressions.

Thank you very much.	You're welcome.
Don't mention it.	My pleasure.
I do beg your pardon.	Sorry to bother you.
How do you do?	If it's not too much trouble.

Times of day are given a linguistic introduction (*Good morning, Good night*), along with their informal variants (*Morning, Night-night*). Unexpected body noises elicit linguistic apologies (*Bless you, Pardon me*). Written English introduces us to special formulae (*Yours sincerely, All the best*). We learn to use the appropriate terms of address for different kinds of people in society (§19). And at the informal end of the scale, different groups develop their own politeness routines (*Hi, Yo, Cheers*).

It's never possible to predict which words and phrases in a language a social group is going to accept or reject as polite. What is clear is that, from age to age, these expressions change. We can see this if we look at some of the expressions Jonathan Swift noted in the early 18th century. He tells us he used to keep a notebook in his pocket when he went to visit the 'most polite families'. After he left the company, he would write down 'the choicest expressions that passed during the visit'. Modern linguists do the same sort of thing as they travel about.

Some of the expressions Swift heard are still with us today. The members of his polite families said such things as *talk of the devil* and *it's an ill wind*. But most of them reflect a past age. A modern ear would make nothing of *You are but just come out of the Cloth-Market* – meaning 'you've just got out of bed'. And although the gist of this extract from Swift's *Polite Conversation* is clear enough, some expressions do require a gloss.

> LADY SMART: Well, Ladies, now let us have a Cup of Discourse to our selves. [a cup of tea and talk]
>
> LADY ANSWERALL: What do you think of your Friend, Sir John *Spendall*?
>
> LADY SMART: Why, Madam, 'tis happy for him that his Father was born before him. [in other words, he isn't thrifty]
>
> MISS NOTABLE: They say, he makes a very ill Husband to my Lady.
>
> LADY ANSWERALL: Well, but he must be allowed to be the fondest Father in the World.
>
> LADY SMART: Ay, Madam, that's true; for they say, the Devil is kind to his own.
>
> MISS NOTABLE: I am told, my Lady manages him to Admiration.
>
> LADY SMART: That I believe, for she's as cunning as a dead Pig; but not half so honest.

Swift points out that the reader will find these phrases extremely helpful, for the expressions can be used over and over on all occasions. He wouldn't find much difference if he were observing polite conversation today. Some things don't change.

Dilly-dally
a reduplicating word (17th century)

English has some ingenious ways of making new vocabulary, but none more so than the technique of taking a word and saying it twice in quick succession – but changing one of the vowels or consonants in the process. The phenomenon is called *reduplication*.

It's something that little children do quite naturally when they're learning to talk. Many of their early words contain a repeated syllable – *mama, dada, baba, bye-bye, night-night, wee-wee* – and soon the reduplication appears with a change in the vowel – *mummy, daddy, baby*. It's a short step from there to doing the same thing with two words. We hear it in many nursery rhymes and fairy stories. Do you remember Chicken Licken, who was so worried that the sky was falling down that he rushed off to tell the king? On the way he met a host of reduplicating friends – Henny Penny, Goosey Loosey, Turkey Lurkey – and, eventually, Foxy Loxy. The names vary in different tellings (such as Hen Len and Goose Loose), but the reduplication is always there.

This is reduplication for fun. The repetition is there to make the names sound appealing, and it also helps children remember the story. Grown-ups reduplicate for other reasons too. Sometimes it's simply to emphasise a meaning, often adding a note of exasperation or criticism. This is what happened to *dally*, which already existed in 16th-century English as a

'WELL-LOVED TALES'

Chicken Licken

A LADYBIRD 'EASY READING' BOOK

11. *A children's story that relies on reduplication for its effect.*

verb meaning 'trifle' or 'delay'. Around the beginning of the 17th century, it was reduplicated. *Stop dilly-dallying!* meant 'Make your mind up!' The same sort of development happened with *shilly-shally*, also expressing the notion of being undecided. This was originally *shill I, shall I*, a stronger version of *shall I, shall I*.

Words like *zig-zag* are created for a different reason. Here there's an attempt to symbolise a shape or movement in the outside world. The contrasting vowels reflect a change in direction. *Zig-zag* originally described a pattern of short, angled lines going in alternate directions, but it was soon used for all kinds of alternating shapes and movements – from lightning to knitting patterns. During the First World War it became a piece of military slang. If you were zig-zag, you were drunk.

Interesting things can happen to these reduplicated words. They can even be broken down into their parts, each one being used as a separate word. We can talk about people *shillying and shallying*. One such usage gained immortality in an old music-hall song:

> My old man said 'Follow the van,
> And don't dilly dally on the way'.
> Off went the van wiv me 'ome packed in it,
> I followed on wiv me old cock linnet.
> But I dillied and dallied, dallied and I dillied,
> Lost me way and don't know where to roam ...

The list of reduplicated words in English is a very

long one. The usual pattern is for the first element to have a vowel high up in the front of the mouth and the second element to have one low down in the back of the mouth. The *i*-to-*a* change is very popular – *pitter-patter, riff-raff, knick-knack, chit-chat* ... So is *i*-to-*o*: *criss-cross, sing-song, ping-pong, tick-tock* ... Another pattern uses a change of consonant, and the two elements rhyme: *helter-skelter, hanky-panky, fuddy-duddy, super-duper* ... Shakespeare evidently liked this kind of word creation, for several examples appear in his plays: *skimble-skamble, bibble-babble, hugger-mugger, hurly-burly* ...

Some reduplications must be quite old. Although *willy-nilly* isn't recorded until the 17th century, its forms reflect a much earlier state of the language – *will I, nill I*, where *nill* is Old English, a conflation of *ne* and *will*, meaning 'will not'. And they evidently remain popular, as new reduplications continue to be created. Since the 1970s we've had *hip-hop, happy-clappy* and *oogly-boogly*. Oogly-boogly? Something scary that jumps out at you in a horror film. Remember the monster that bursts out of the chest of Kane (John Hurt) in *Alien*? That was an oogly-boogly.

Rep
a clipping (17th century)

If you're a *rep*, what are you? In the 17th century, you weren't one: you had one. *Rep* was short for *reputation*. People would say something *upon rep*, meaning, 'I'll stake my reputation on it'.

In the late 1600s it was linguistically fashionable to shorten words in this way. People didn't say *incognito* in casual speech, but *incog*. They said *That's pos* or *pozz* for *positive* – meaning 'That's certain'. And they talked about a crowd of people as a *mob*. That was a two-stage shortening. *Mobile vulgus*, meaning 'fickle crowd', had come into English at the end of the 16th century. During the next century it was first shortened to *mobile*, and then to *mob*.

Words which are reduced in size in this way are called *clippings*. The essayist Joseph Addison couldn't stand them. In an issue of the *Spectator* in 1711 he complained about the way people have 'miserably curtailed some of our Words', and he cites all the above. (It didn't stop him using *pozz* himself, a few years later, though.)

Clippings are very common in the history of English. The ends of words are clipped in *ad*, *celeb*, *doc* and *prof*. The beginnings go in *phone* and *burger*. And both beginning and end go in *flu* and *fridge*. They are typically informal in style, but in many cases the clipping has lost its informal tone and become the regular expression, with the full form perceived as more formal or precise: think of the full forms of *fax, memo, gym, exam, vet, pub* and *flu.* In some cases, such as *bus* and *cello,* the original full form (*omnibus, violoncello*) is hardly ever used. With *mob,* never.

Just because a word is clipped doesn't stop it changing in meaning, of course, and the history of *rep* illustrates the point perfectly. In the 18th century it became a shortened form of *reprobate* – an immoral or dissolute person. A woman with a doubtful reputation was a *demi-rep.* At the same time, the clipping appeared with a capital *R,* first for *Republic,* then for a member of the House of *Representatives* (in the US political system) and in the 19th century for a member of the *Republican* Party.

The 20th century saw further developments. From around 1900 *rep* (for *repertory*) became the normal way of referring to a theatre company that put on a regular programme of plays. Actors appeared *in repertory,* or *in rep.* Then, during the century, *reps* turned up as *representatives* of all kinds of organisations. *Holiday reps* looked after you when you travelled. *Union reps* looked after their members. *Sales reps* tried to sell you things.

Since the 1930s, *rep* has also been short for *repetitions.* Instructions to perform an activity repeatedly are a routine part of many sport or health programmes. *Twenty reps. Fifty reps.* How many reps does it take to strengthen a muscle? Body-builders know.

Americanism

a new nation (18th century)

The United States hadn't been born five years before the word *Americanism* was invented. It was coined by John Witherspoon, a Scottish minister who had become president of the College of New Jersey. Writing in a Pennsylvania journal in 1781, he says he made the word up on analogy with *Scotticism*. Any usage different from what was used in Britain he would henceforth call an *Americanism*.

The word caught on and was soon applied to everything American – behaviour, customs and institutions. It was all part of the process of forging a new national identity. When Noah Webster compiled his *Compendious Dictionary* in 1806, he emphasised the word's general meaning, defining it as a 'love of America and preference of her interest'.

This was the first dictionary to contain words specific to the USA. We find in its pages such local items as *butternut, caucus, checkers, chowder, constitutionality, hickory, opossum, skunk* and *succotash*. And we see the first sign of the spelling innovations which would soon become the hallmark of American English, such as *color* and *defense*.

Two hundred years on, a dictionary of Americanisms would be large indeed, especially if regional variations in usage were included. The five volumes of the great *Dictionary of American Regional English* contain several thousand entries. What words do

12. *The British and American covers of this book in the Harry Potter series show how linguistic and cultural differences can affect even titles. The linguistic contrasts include idiomatic expressions as well as single words: 'Bit rich coming from you!' says British Harry to British Ron in Chapter 2 of* The Chamber of Secrets. *'You should talk!' says American Harry to American Ron.*

people use for a strip of grass between the sidewalk (in Britain: *pavement*) and the street? The research team found *boulevard, devil strip, grass plot, neutral ground, parking, parking strip, parkway, terrace, tree bank, tree belt, tree lawn* and many more.

Leaving aside regionalisms, British and American English display hundreds of differences. Take the words for the parts of a car. British terms include *wing mirror, number plate, petrol cap, aerial, windscreen, wing, bonnet* and *boot*. The American equivalents are *side-view mirror, license plate, gas cap, antenna, windshield, fender, hood* and *trunk*. Abbreviations can cause a problem. Some, such as *CNN* and *BBC*, have travelled across the Atlantic. Others, such as *ATT* and *BT*, haven't. British people need to be told about the American Telephone and Telegraph Company; Americans, likewise, about British Telecom.

Idioms can be a problem too. Most British people know next to nothing about baseball, so they look blank when they hear about a company that has *hit a home run* ('been very successful'). Similarly, most Americans know next to nothing about cricket, so they look blank when they hear about a politician *batting on a sticky wicket* ('having a difficult time'). Sometimes there are neat equivalents: if someone is *caught off base*, that's baseball's equivalent to cricket's *caught out*.

Many American words are familiar in the UK now, thanks to the prevalence of American TV shows and movies. My five-year-old grandson is already well versed in *faucets* ('taps'), *drapes* ('curtains') and *railroads* ('railways'), thanks to repeated exposure to Mickey Mouse, Special Agent Oso and other inhabitants of the Disney Channel. I doubt whether American five-year-olds would be so well versed in the equivalent British English words. British English tends to get translated.

Not even Harry Potter is immune. In the British editions, the children eat *crumpets* and *crisps*; in the US editions they eat *English muffins* and *chips*. *Cookers* become *stoves*, *dustbins* become *trashcans* and *jumpers* become *sweaters*. But some differences are more cultural than linguistic. In the UK, one of the books was called *Harry Potter and the Philosopher's Stone*. In the USA, *Philosopher* was replaced by *Sorcerer*.

59 *Edit*

a back-formation (18th century)

'Which came first?' is the daily question when exploring the history of words. Normally, we find that words build up in size over time. We find *nation* in the 1300s, then *national* in the 1500s, then *nationalise* in the 1700s, then *nationalisation* in the 1800s, along with *denationalisation* – and doubtless *antidenationalisation* is out there somewhere now. That's the expected pattern. So *edit* comes as a bit of a surprise, because there the pattern is the other way round.

We start with *edition* in the 1500s. A century later

we find *editor*, and a century after that *editorship*. So far, so normal. Then, in the 1790s, along comes *edit*. The verb was formed by dropping the ending from *editor*. Linguists call such things *back-formations*.

Back-formations have been in the language a long time, but they seem to have increased in popularity over the past 200 years. Along with *edit* in the 18th century came *swindle* (from *swindler*) and *gamble* (from *gambler*). In the 19th we find such formations as *shoplift* (from *shoplifter*) and *sculpt* (from *sculptor*). In the 20th there was *automate* (from *automation*), *babysit* (from *babysitter*), *televise* (from *television*) and dozens more. It can take quite a while for a back-formation to surface. *Burglar* is there in the 13th century, but we don't find *burgle* until the 1870s. *Housekeeper* dates from the 1440s; to *housekeep* only appears 400 years later. On the other hand, when *staycation* arrived in the 2000s, for a 'stay-at-home vacation', one concerned travel firm immediately introduced the slogan: *Why staycate when you can vacate?*

Not all back-formations are immediately accepted. Among the usages which have attracted criticism are *helicopt*, *caretake* and *therap*. Would you like to be *helicopted*? *Helicoptered* seems to be the preferred form. But the naturalness of back-formation is clear from the way people are very ready to make jocular coinages. I've often heard people say that someone was being *couth* (as opposed to *uncouth*). *Shevelled* and *sipid*? Not *dishevelled* or *inspid*. And the opposite of *disgruntled*? *Gruntled*, of course (a P. G. Wodehouse innovation).

Slightly off the topic, but worth reporting as an end-note. I don't know if I'd come across *editress* before, as the feminine form of *editor*, but I found it in my trawl through the history of *edit*. It seems to have been quite popular in the 19th century. So was *editrix*. Neither one has died out. There are several web sites with *editress* or *editrix* in the title. I suspect that most of them are tongue-in-cheek.

 ## *Species*
classifying things (18th century)

How many words are there in the English language? It's one of those impossible questions to answer, because it partly depends on what you count as a word. Is *flower pot* one word or two? And *washing machine*? Do all abbreviations count as words? How many words are there in *Meet me at 4 pm outside your HQ for a G&T*? And what are we to do with the thousands of Latin and Greek words used in classifying the natural world?

Some 2 million species of living things have been described using the naming system devised by Carolus Linnaeus in the 18th century. This was a system where plants and animals are first identified as belonging to a particular *species*; species are then grouped into types called *genera* (singular form, *genus*); and genera are grouped into *families*. Most of the time, a genus and a species are enough to identify what someone is talking about.

For example, the various species of tulip belong to the genus *Tulipa*, which along with other genera (such as daffodils and lilies) makes up the family *Liliaceae*. Different species are then distinguished as *Tulipa sylvestris* ('woodland tulip'), *Tulipa clusiana* ('lady tulip') and so on. Similarly, the various species of cat belong to the genus *Felis*, which along with other genera (such as tigers and cheetahs) makes up the family *Felidae*. Different species are distinguished as *Felis catus* ('domestic cat'), *Felis sylvestris* ('wild cat') and so on, then further distinguished as breeds, such as *Felis catus siamensis* ('Siamese cat') and *Felis catus anura* ('Manx cat').

These are all technical terms, intended to replace the vagueness in everyday names. The name *bluebell* refers to different plants in England and Scotland, and of course has a totally different name when translated into other languages. But the Latin term is always used in the same way, so gardeners in every country can understand each other more easily, and ambiguity is avoided. Most people don't use the full descriptions, though anyone wanting to be taken seriously as a botanist would have to know some of them.

Do all these classical names count as English? We can't ignore them. In a discussion at a flower show, we will often hear such sentences as 'I've got a large clump of *Tulipa tarda* in my garden, and it looks terrific', and several of the technical names have actually become everyday usage, such as *rhododendron* and *fuchsia*. Similarly, any walk around a zoo or a natural history museum will introduce us to the technical names of animals, some of which, such as *Homo sapiens* ('wise human') and *Tyrannosaurus rex* ('tyrant lizard king'), have become widely known.

If there are 2 million known species, then there are 2 million names awaiting inclusion in a super-dictionary. And we ain't seen nothin' yet, for biologists say that many more millions of species have yet to be discovered.

 ## 61 *Ain't*
right and wrong (18th century)

For a word that has regularly attracted a bad press during the 20th century, *ain't* is remarkably audible in speech and visible in writing. It's widely condemned as bad English, and yet all kinds of people use it. It isn't just something we hear in regional dialect speech. Speakers of standard English use it too, in such expressions as *If it ain't broke don't fix it, Ain't it the truth, Ready it ain't* and *Things ain't what they used to be*. They're using the non-standard form to make their speech sound more robust, unpretentious and down-to-earth.

We'll also find it in written English. Did you notice

an example at the end of the previous chapter? It's by no means the first time that the expression has been used in print. Indeed, in 2002 it was part of a book title: *You Ain't Seen Nothing Yet: The Future of Media and the Global Expert System*. And several other titles have included an *ain't*, such as *Ain't Misbehavin': A Good Behaviour Guide for Family Dogs* and *It Ain't Necessarily So: Investigating the Truth of the Biblical Past*. The non-standard form, unusual in print, grabs the attention.

In these last two cases there's an allusion to a well-known song. We seem to have stored away in our memory such phrases as *ain't misbehavin'* (the name of a Louis Armstrong hit from the 1929 musical comedy *Hot Chocolates*) and can bring them out again as required, confident that other people will recognise the allusions. Nor is it only song that uses the word. *It Ain't Half Hot, Mum* has entered British consciousness as a result of a popular TV programme. *It ain't over till the fat lady sings* has prompted a sports commentary cliché.

Ain't has had an unusual history. It's a shortened form of several words – *am not, are not, is not, has not* and *have not*. It appears in written English in the 18th century in various plays and novels, first as *an't* and then as *ain't*. During the 19th century it was widely used in representations of regional dialect, especially Cockney speech in the UK, and became a distinctive feature of colloquial American English. But when we look at who is using the form in 19th-century novels, such as those by Dickens and Trollope, we find that the characters are often professional and upper-class. That's unusual: to find a form simultaneously used at both ends of the social spectrum. Even as recently as 1907, in a commentary on society called *The Social Fetich*, Lady Agnes Grove was defending *ain't I* as respectable upper-class colloquial speech – and condemning *aren't I*!

She was in a rapidly diminishing minority. Prescriptive grammarians had taken against *ain't*, and it would soon become universally condemned as a leading marker of uneducated usage. There was a chorus of criticism in 1961 when the editor of *Webster's Third New International Dictionary* decided it was so widespread, even among cultivated speakers, that he could not possibly omit it. Rarely has a single word attracted such fury. But, as *gotcha* and other non-standard spellings illustrate, it's by no means alone (§88).

Trek
a word from Africa (19th century)

In 1883, Olive Schreiner published a novel in London under the pseudonym of Ralph Iron. It was called *The Story of an African Farm* – a tale about a strong, independent-minded woman working on an isolated ostrich farm. The first novel to come out of South Africa, it became a bestseller.

While she was writing her book, Schreiner knew

she had a problem. How was she to present the South African setting in an intelligible way? The opening lines of her story paint a picture of the countryside. It talks about *karroo bushes, kopjes* and *sheep kraals*. How would British readers know what she was talking about?

Her solution was to put a glossary of the most important words at the front of the book. There the reader would learn that the *karroo* was a 'wide sandy plain', a *kopje* was 'a small hillock' and a *kraal* was 'the space surrounded by a stone wall or hedged with thorn branches, into which sheep or cattle are driven at night'. The words included animals (*meerkat*, 'a small weasel-like animal'), people (*predikant*, 'parson'), food (*bultong*, 'dried meat'), clothing (*kappje*, 'a sun-bonnet') and various domestic objects and activities. Most of the words were of Afrikaans origin, but some were adaptations of British words. An *upsitting*, for instance, was a custom in Boer courtship: 'the man and girl are supposed to sit up together the whole night.'

It was during the 19th century that words from Africa began to make an impact on English vocabulary. Previously, there had been very few. *Yam* and *banana* had arrived during the 16th century, and a few more followed, such as *harmattan* (a type of wind) and *zebra*. In South Africa, *kraal* appears in the 18th century, first in the sense of 'village', then in Schreiner's sense of 'animal enclosure'. Hundreds of words remained local to South Africa, such as *bioscope* ('cinema') and *dorp* ('village'), along with borrowings from indigenous languages, such as *maningi* ('very') and *induna* ('headman'). Several became part of standard English, such as *commando, spoor* and *veld*, as well as politically loaded terms such as *resettlement* and *apartheid*. But few have achieved such general usage as *trek*.

Trek arrived in the 1840s, meaning a journey by ox-wagon, very much associated with Boer movements in the region following the first 'Great Trek'. It developed several senses in South African English and came to be used in a number of compounds, such as *trek path* ('right of way') and *trek swarm* ('migrating honey bees'). But a century later, it was being used for any arduous overland journey in any part of the world. It became the perfect media word to describe dramatic explorations of jungles, deserts and ice caps.

Then *trek* went in a different direction. People began to use it for activities which, in Boer terms, would have seemed totally trivial. A boring or routine trip to the shops was called a *trek*. People *trekked* from home to their offices. *Trekking* holidays became popular, with *trekkers* warned to choose a level of physical commitment they could cope with. It didn't even have to be a physical task. You could go on a *mental trek*, if you were going on an emotional journey or having difficulty thinking something out.

In the 1960s, there was an unpredictable development: a use developed with a capital *T*. Devotees of a new science fiction television series came to be called *Trekkies* or *Trekkers* (the choice was serious, as each name had its supporters and critics). In 1997 a documentary film about the fans was called *Trekkies*. The term began to be used beyond the series: anyone obsessed with fantasy space travel might be labelled a *trekkie* (with a small *t*). Thanks to *Star Trek*, the word has regained its 'long-distance' meaning, boldly going where no loanword has gone before.

 # *Hello*

progress through technology (19th century)

It's such a natural expression, used every day as a greeting. Surely this is one of those words which has been in the language for ever? In fact, its first recorded use is less than 200 years old.

English people have been using *h*-words to catch each other's attention since Anglo-Saxon times. *Hey* and *ho* are recorded in the 13th century, and *hi* in the 15th. *Hollo, hillo, holla, halloo* and other shouts used in hunting are known from the 16th century, and are doubtless much older. For greetings, one of the words used by the Anglo-Saxons was *hal* ('whole', 'healthy') in such expressions as 'be healthy'. *Hail* appeared in the 13th century. But we have to wait until the 19th century to see the modern greeting.

When it emerges, we find it in several spellings. All five vowels are used: *hallo, hello, hillo, hollo* and

13. An early advertisement for Bell Telephones in the USA, emphasising the social role of the phone in a family context. When the telephone first arrived, there was a degree of concern that it might herald the end of traditional face-to-face social interaction. Ads like this one were intended to counter that scepticism.

hullo. The variations arose because the stress in the word was on the second syllable, making it difficult to hear the quality of the vowel in the first. Today, *hello* is the usual spelling, about four times more common than *hallo* – except when authors are putting words into the mouths of policemen: *Hallo, 'allo, 'allo* says PC Palk, answering the phone in Agatha Christie's *The Body in the Library*.

Why did *hello* catch on? The word was around in the early 1800s, but used very informally, often as a part of street slang. The more formal usage seems to have emerged when the telephone was invented. People had to have a way of starting a conversation or letting the other person know they were there, especially if they were using a line where the connection was always open. Various forms were suggested, such as *Ahoy!, Are you there?* and *Are you ready?*, but Thomas Edison, the inventor of the telephone, evidently preferred *Hello*. This was the word he shouted into the mouthpiece of his device when he discovered a way of recording sound in 1877. And there is a famous letter which he wrote to a colleague about the telephone saying, 'I do not think we shall need a call bell as Hello! can be heard 10 to 20 feet away.' Within a decade, the women who were employed as the first telephone operators were being called *hello girls*.

Hello illustrates how technology can influence vocabulary, pushing a word in a new direction. Other uses continue to emerge, of course. In particular,

since the 1980s *hello* has developed an ironic atten-
tion-getting use, implying that someone has failed to
understand or has missed the point in some way: 'I
mean, hello! How crazy was that?' But its future as an
informal greeting is being seriously challenged by *Hi*,
which emerged in the USA in the 19th century. *Hi* is
now heard globally across the age range – though it's
rather less widespread among older people, where
hello is still the norm – and has become frequent
in written English too. It's the commonest way of
beginning an email to someone we know. Two letters
are quicker to type than five, no matter how old you
are. Technology rules, once again.

Dragsman
thieves' cant (19th century)

Dictionaries chiefly deal in the words used by the
great and the good. Dr Johnson started a trend when
he paid special attention in his *Dictionary* entries to
the cultured usage of the best authors, 'the wells of
English undefiled'. There's little sign in his pages of
the everyday slang of ordinary people – and certainly
no coverage of the secretive usage (often called *cant*,
or *argot*) of criminals. But villains have vocabulary
too.

It's not easy to study, though. If we wanted to
collect the words used by criminals and establish
their senses, we would have to enter their world and

stay for quite some time. A risky business. But some intrepid lexicographers have done precisely that.

One of the first was George Andrewes, who compiled *A Dictionary of the Slang and Cant Languages* in 1809. He had a highly practical aim in mind. Thieves have a language of their own, he says, so that when they get together in the streets passers-by won't understand what they're plotting. His *Dictionary*, he hopes, will make it easier to detect their crimes: 'by the perusal of this Work, the Public will become acquainted with their mysterious Phrases; and be better able to frustrate their designs.'

Dragsmen were one of the types of villain he had in mind. In the 18th century, a *drag* was a private horse-drawn vehicle similar to a stage coach, with seats inside and on the top. A *dragsman* was its driver. But the term was also used for someone who stole ('dragged') goods or luggage from vehicles. They were also called *draggers*, for obvious reasons. *Drag* went out of use for the name of a vehicle once the motor car was invented; but it surfaced again in the 1950s when the American sport of *drag racing* developed (initially along the *drag*, or main street, of a town).

Andrewes provides a long list of names for the different kinds of criminal activity. Some, such as *footpads* and *coiners* ('counterfeiters'), are still used today. *Fencer* is close to what we now say for a receiver of stolen goods (a *fence*). And we might guess what a *water-pad* is, on analogy with *footpad*. Someone who robs ships.

Several of the unfamiliar names are highly descriptive. A *cloak-twitcher*, as its form suggests, was someone who would lurk in a dark place and snatch a cloak from the shoulders of its wearer. A *beau-trap* was a well-dressed confidence trickster. A *diver* was a pickpocket. Others are less transparent, and their origins aren't known. Housebreakers were *kencrackers*, from an old slang term for a house, *ken*, but where that word comes from nobody knows. A *prigger* was a thief. A *lully-prigger* was a linen-thief. Nobody knows where these words come from either.

Two of the most puzzling terms listed by Andrewes are *clapperdogeons* and *gammoners*. A *clapperdogeon* – also spelled *clapperdudgeon* – was a beggar. It seems to be a combination of *clapper* ('lid of a begging dish') and *dudgeon* ('hilt of a dagger'). Maybe beggars knocked the lid of their dish with it. A *gammoner* was a pickpocket's accomplice – someone who held the attention of the target while a pocket was picked. *Give me gammon*, the pickpocket might say to the accomplice. Maybe *gammon* comes from *game*, in its sense of a 'scheme' or 'intrigue' – we still say such things as *so that's your little game* and *two can play at that game*. Or could there be an obscure link with the game of backgammon ('back-game')? Again, nobody knows.

Lunch
U or non-U (19th century)

What do you call the meal you have in the middle of the day? For many readers, there is no question: *lunch*. For many readers, there is no question: *dinner*. Clearly, there's an issue here, and it's one that has been a feature of English vocabulary for a long time.

In Britain, the issue was highlighted in the 1950s, when considerable media attention was paid to the vocabulary differences between upper-class (or 'U') speakers and those belonging to other classes ('non-U'). It was claimed that U speakers said *lunch* or *luncheon*; everyone else said *dinner*. And similarly, U-speakers were supposed to say *vegetables, lavatory paper* and *bike*; non-U speakers *greens, toilet paper* and *cycle*. Long lists were compiled to illustrate the supposed linguistic 'class war'.

The situation was never as neat and tidy as the distinction suggested. U-speakers certainly called their midday meal *lunch(eon)*, but if they had a dog they would give it its *dinner* at that time of day. One didn't invite one's dog to take lunch. Similarly, U-children would also be summoned to *dinner*, especially in school, where the meal in the middle of the day would be served by *dinner ladies*. Most *Christmas dinners* were eaten in the early afternoon. So were *Thanksgiving dinners*. And the words sometimes went in the opposite direction. Businessmen having an evening meal in a restaurant might nonetheless pay for it with *luncheon vouchers*.

The words have gone backwards and forwards in recent centuries. Originally, there was only *dinner* – a word that arrived from French in the 13th century to describe the chief meal of the day. This was usually eaten around midday – as is clear from many observations. In Shakespeare's *As You Like It* (IV.i.166), Orlando tells Rosalind he has to leave her for two hours: 'I must attend the Duke at dinner. By two o'clock I will be with thee again.' It was the same in the 18th century. James Boswell, in his *Life of Johnson*, writes of being invited to 'dinner at two'.

The words *luncheon* and *lunch* both arrived in the late 16th century, though not in their modern sense. A *lunch(eon)* was a thick piece of food – a hunk of something. People would talk about 'a luncheon of cheese' or 'a lunch of bacon'. Then *luncheon* began to move in the direction of its modern meaning. In the 17th century, it was a light repast taken between the main meals. There would be breakfast, then luncheon, then (midday) dinner; or, dinner, then luncheon, then supper. In the 1820s Thomas Carlyle writes about an *evening luncheon*. And in the USA there are instances of luncheons being served as late as midnight.

The modern usage of *lunch* isn't recorded until 1829, and not everyone liked it. Some considered it a vulgar abbreviation; others, a ridiculous affectation. At the same time, *luncheon* was attracting criticism as a word unsuitable for use in high society. But *dinner* was also being frowned upon, because of its growing lower-class associations. So what should people say? There were some strange coinages as they searched for a solution. *Lunch-dinner* is recorded a few times during the century, as are *luncheon-dinner* and *dinner-supper*. It must all have been very confusing.

Eventually, as we now know, the present-day use of *lunch* and *dinner* became established among the fashionable classes. As the 20th century dawned, the pages of *Punch* magazine are full of references to business *lunches* and evening *dinner* parties. Meanwhile, the lower orders of society continued to use *dinner* for their midday meal, and so the U/non-U distinction was born. But the story of *lunch* and *dinner* is not over yet. Expressions such as *lunch-box* and *packed lunch* have reinforced a change of usage among many non-U children, so that they now happily talk about *school lunches* (though still served by dinner ladies). However, when chef Jamie Oliver started his campaign on British television in 2005 for more nutritious food in school lunches, he called it *Jamie's School Dinners*.

Dude
a cool usage (19th century)

Dude is another word whose origin is unknown. All we know is that it suddenly appeared in 1883 in New

York. The London newspaper *The Graphic* reported its arrival in March of that year as 'American slang for a new kind of American young man'. A couple of months later, the *North Adams Transcript* of Massachusetts confirmed its spread: 'The new coined word "dude" ... has travelled over the country with a great deal of rapidity since but two months ago it grew into general use in New York.' Rarely do we find such a precise dating of a word (§83). But who coined it, and why, remains a mystery.

Dudes were aesthetes and dandies – any man who was extremely fastidious about his clothes, speech and general behaviour. They often dressed in a British way and affected a British tone of voice. If you were clothed like a dude, you were *duded up*. But soon the word began to extend its meaning. Any city-dweller who went 'out West' as a tourist would be called a dude. *Dude ranches* developed to cater for the demand from city dudes. And it wasn't long before the female dude was identified – and given a name: *dudess* or *dudine*, though neither of these words has survived.

By the turn of the century, anyone who stood out in a crowd was being called a dude. In small-group settings, such as school classrooms, street gangs and jazz clubs, it became a term of approval. Eventually any group of people hanging out together would refer to themselves as dudes. It became one of a large number of 'cool' slang terms for people, such as *cat* (in the jazz world) and *geek* (in the computer world).

By the 1970s *dude* had become a chatty term of address for both men and women, especially popular in American university campuses and often heard in high school and college movies. *Bill and Ted's Excellent Adventure* (1989) contained such famous lines as 'All we are is dust in the wind, dude!' and 'How's it goin', royal ugly dudes?' Bill and Ted's teacher, Mr Ryan, is unimpressed by the usage.

> Mr Ryan: So Bill, what you're telling me, essentially, is that Napoleon was a short, dead dude.
>
> Bill: Well, yeah.
>
> Ted (to Bill): You totally blew it, dude.

Brunch
a portmanteau word (19th century)

We know the year that *brunch* entered the English language. According to the satirical magazine *Punch*, it was 1895. This is what a writer in August 1896 had to say about it:

> To be fashionable nowadays we must 'brunch'. Truly an excellent portmanteau word, introduced, by the way, last year, by Mr. Guy Beringer, in the now defunct *Hunter's Weekly*, and indicating a combined breakfast and lunch.

Indeed he did. Beringer's article, 'Brunch: A Plea', proposed an alternative to the Sunday 'postchurch ordeal of heavy meats and savoury pies'. Brunch, said Beringer, 'puts you in a good temper, it makes you satisfied with yourself and your fellow beings, it sweeps away the worries and cobwebs of the week'.

There certainly is a quirky freshness about the name, which is still with us. It caught on, and by the 1930s the noun was also being used as a verb: 'I brunched with Jim', someone might say. We also find it being used to make compound words, such as *brunch-style* and *brunch box*. In the 1940s, a type of women's short house-coat was called a *brunch coat*. By the 1960s a new kind of eating-house had emerged: the *brunch-bar*. And Cadbury used that name for a chocolate-covered cereal bar.

The *Punch* writer called *brunch* a portmanteau word. A *portmanteau*, as its French origin suggests, was a small case which a horse-rider could use to carry (*porter* = 'to carry') a cloak (*manteau*) or other clothes or belongings. But it changed its meaning in the late 19th century, after Lewis Carroll used it in *Through the Looking-Glass* (1871) to explain his coinages in 'Jabberwocky'. *Slithy*, says Humpty Dumpty, 'means *lithe* and *slimy* ... it's like a portmanteau – there are two meanings packed up into one word'. Today, linguists tend to call such words *blends* – but there is something rather appealing about Lewis Carroll's usage which has kept the older term in vogue.

The meaning of a portmanteau word is different

from the sum of its parts. *Brunch* isn't two meals – breakfast and lunch – but a meal that is different from either. And this is the pattern we find in all portmanteau words. A *spork* is neither a spoon nor a fork, but a new device that mixes properties of both. A *motorcade* is not a motor car nor a cavalcade, but a new kind of procession.

Portmanteaus have been part of the English language for centuries. *Tragicomedy* dates from the 16th century; *Oxbridge* from the 19th. But blending became one of the most popular ways of coining new words during the 20th century. *Spork* is first recorded in 1909 and *motorcade* in 1913, and hundreds of others followed – such as *gasohol, internet, interpol, motel, chocoholic, docusoap* and *guestimate*. Informal English has a special liking for them – *fantabulous, ginormous, happenstance*. The process is especially popular today (§98).

Some of the most unusual blends appear in house-names – if Derek and Susan set up house together, they might call their place *Dersan* or *Suerek*. And the tabloid media love to join the names of famous couples together in a personal portmanteau. Who was/were *Brangelina*? Brad Pitt and Angelina Jolie. And who was/were *Bennifer*? Ben Affleck and Jennifer Lopez. Whether the whole is different from the sum of the parts, in such cases, is a moot point.

68 *Dinkum*
a word from Australia (19th century)

On 29 April 1770, Captain Cook arrived in Australia. Two months later he writes in his journal: 'One of the Men saw an Animal something less than a grey-hound; it was of a Mouse Colour, very slender made, and swift of Foot.' They soon learned its local name. Cook writes on 4th August: 'called by the Natives Kangooroo, or Kanguru'. It was the first of many words that would eventually become a feature of Australian English.

The aboriginal languages of the region supplied some of the most distinctive items. Local animals, landscape and culture are reflected in *billabong, dingo, koala, wombat, budgerigar, kookaburra* and *boomerang*. Less distinctive, but more numerous, were words from British English used in new ways. A *paddock* in Britain was a small animal enclosure; now it described a vast tract of rural land. *Swag* was a slang word for a thief's booty; it came to mean a bundle of personal belongings carried by a traveller in the bush. A *footpath* is paved in Australia – what in Britain would be a *pavement* and in the USA a *sidewalk*.

Bush itself was one of these changes of sense, referring to the huge expanse of natural countryside that formed inland Australia. It became the basis of a wide range of expressions, such as *bush mouse* and *bush turkey, bush cucumber* and *bush tomato, bush ballad* and *bush medicine*. Few have travelled outside

Australia. An exception is *bush telegraph*, meaning the rapid spread of news or rumours.

Words from British regional dialects often underlie an Australian usage. *Dinkum* is a case in point. This is one of the best-known Australianisms, especially in the phrase *fair dinkum*. It appears in the 19th century in Britain, and is recorded by Joseph Wright in his *English Dialect Dictionary*. He found *dinkum* in Derbyshire and *fair dinkum* in Lincolnshire. *Dinkum* meant 'hard work', and *fair dinkum* was your 'fair share of work'.

These senses travelled to Australia, but soon developed more general meanings of 'honest, genuine' and 'good, excellent', which is how the word is used today. Its popularity is suggested by the way it developed alternative forms, shortening to *dink* and lengthening to *dinki-di*. The origin of the word isn't known. There are other uses, such as *dink* meaning 'finely dressed' and *dinky* meaning 'neat, small', all with a history in British dialects, but it's difficult to see how they relate to the Australian use.

Thanks to the international popularity of Australian films and TV programmes, the English-speaking world has come to be familiar with *dinkum* and other informal expressions such as *cobber* ('mate'), *pom* ('British person'), *sheila* ('woman'), *tucker* ('food') and *g'day* (as a greeting), as well as abbreviated forms such as *beaut* (as a term of praise) and *arvo* ('afternoon'). Just occasionally, a colloquialism becomes part of international informal English.

Barbies ('barbecues') have been with us since the 1970s.

The down side of media presence is that it often paints an exaggerated picture of Australian English. Outsiders hear colourful phrases and assume that everyone talks in the same way. Books of Australianisms have collected such expressions as *miserable as a bandicoot, flat out like a lizard drinking* and *he couldn't find a grand piano in a one-roomed house*, but it's debatable just how many people have actually ever used them.

69 *Mipela*
pidgin English (19th century)

You won't find *mipela* or *mifela* in a dictionary of standard English, but these words belong to the language nonetheless – used in different varieties of pidgin English. *Mipela* is one of the pronouns used in the pidgin language of Papua New Guinea called Tok Pisin ('Pidgin Talk'). People generally have a low opinion of pidgin languages. They think of them as primitive compared with standard English, with little or no grammar and a tiny vocabulary.

In fact, a pidgin like Tok Pisin is startlingly sophisticated. Its vocabulary is large enough to cope with translations of the Bible and Shakespeare. And sometimes its expression is more subtle than standard English. The standard pronoun system is pretty

. A sign in Tok Pisin in Papua New Guinea. It reads: 'Beware of cattle', *rally 'look out'* + *'for'* + *'bull and cow'*. Long *is a general-purpose position with functions expressing such notions as 'in', 'of', and 'on'. ; a shortened form of* belong. *When Prince Charles visited Papua New inea in 1966 he was described locally as* nambawan pikinini bilong *sis* kwin *('the number one child of Mrs Queen'). Princess Anne, respondingly, was the* nambawan gel *('girl')* pikinini bilong misis *'in.*

simple, really. We have first person *I* (for singular) and *we* (for plural). Second person is *you* for both singular and plural. Third person is *he, she* or *it* (for singular) and *they* (for plural). It's not the best of systems. *You*, in particular, is ambiguous. If I say *I'm talking to you*, it's not possible to tell whether I'm addressing one person or several.

Tok Pisin does much better. It has four different ways of saying 'you'. *Yu*, on its own, means I'm talking to one person. If I'm talking to two people, I say *yutupela* ('you two'). If I'm talking to three people, I say *yutripela* ('you three'). And if I'm talking to more than three people, I say *yupela*.

The same system operates for the third person. If I say *em*, I mean 'he, she or it'. If I say *tupela*, I mean 'they two'. *Tripela* means 'they three'. And *ol* means 'they four or more'.

The first person is even more sophisticated, as, in addition to *mi* ('I'), Tok Pisin allows speakers to distinguish how many people are included in the conversation. Imagine John and Mary talking to a group. John says, 'We're going to be late'. Does he mean 'Mary and I are going to be late' or 'All of us are going to be late'? In English, it isn't possible to decide without further exploration. In Tok Pisin, however, the distinction is clear. If John meant 'one of you and me', he would say *yumitupela*. If he meant 'two of you and me', he would say *yumitripela*. And if he meant 'all of you and me', he would say *yumipela*.

But he could do something else. He could also

say, addressing Mary, *mitupela*, which would mean 'he or she and me, but not you'. If he said *mitripela*, it would mean 'both of them and me, but not you'. And if he said *mipela*, he would mean 'all of them and me, but not you'. Here he is excluding Mary, whereas with the examples in the previous paragraph he was including her. Standard English has nothing like this. All it has is the highly ambiguous *we*.

The vocabulary of the pidgin Englishes of the world contain tens of thousands of words. Many have a spelling which shows a clear link with the source language, such as *kap* ('cup') and *galas* ('glass'). Other words are more difficult to interpret, such as *liklik* ('little') and *wantaim* ('together'). Taken as a whole, along with the distinctive grammar and pronunciation, some analysts consider the differences from standard English to be so great that they think of pidgin Englishes as new languages. If they're right, we now have an English 'family of languages' on earth.

 # *Schmooze*
a Yiddishism (19th century)

It's the initial two sounds that give *schmooze* away as a Yiddish word. English words traditionally don't allow the sound *sh* to appear before a consonant. A combination of *s* + consonant is fine, as in *spin, still* and *skin*. But if anyone said *shpin, shtill* and *shkin*, we would think they had a speech defect – or were engaging in a bad imitation of Sean Connery.

Things changed in the late 19th century, when a new kind of loanword arrived from Yiddish. English previously had borrowed few words from this language – *matzo* ('unleavened bread') was a very early one, first recorded in 1650. But we don't find much evidence of them in writing until the 19th century, when we get such words as *kibosh* ('finishing off', 1836), *nosh* ('food', 1873) *chutzpah* ('brazen impudence', 1892), *pogrom* ('organised massacre', 1891) – and *schmooze* ('leisurely intimate chat', 1897).

Schmooze wasn't alone as the century turned. Apart from its derived forms (*schmoozer, schmoozing*), it was accompanied by several other words beginning with *schl-* or *schm-*, such as *schlemiel* ('clumsy person') and *schmuck* ('objectionable person'). During the 1920s and '30s we find *schlep* ('haul, toil') and its related forms, such as *schlepping* and *schlepper* ('person of little worth, scrounger'), *schnozzle* and *schnozz* ('nose') and *schmaltz* ('melted chicken fat'), *schmaltzy* and *schmaltziness*, whose 'greasy' connotations led to the word coming to mean 'excessive sentimentality', especially when talking about writing, music and song. *Schm-* in particular seems to have caught on, because by the end of the decade we find it being used in a remarkable way, forming nonsense words.

'There's a crisis,' says one person, and another disagrees. 'Crisis-schmisis!' The usage conveys

scepticism, disparagement or derision. There's
no crisis, and the first speaker is stupid to suggest
there is one. It's a simple sound substitution, and it
became hugely popular, especially in the USA. Spelling varies, with words often appearing with *shm-*, but
all kinds of words have been modified in this way,
as in *surveillance-shmurveillance, marathon-schmarathon,
fancy-shmancy, baby-schmaby* and *holiday-schmoliday*. It
even led to a proper name. *Joe Schmoe* is a fictitious
name for the ordinary American guy.

OK

debatable origins (19th century)

The little word *OK* has a linguistic reputation that
belies its size. Over a thousand words in English
have an etymology which, in the words of the *Oxford
English Dictionary*, is 'origin unknown'. Nobody
knows where *bloke* comes from, or *condom, gimmick,
nifty, pimp, pooch, queasy, rogue* or *skiffle*. Theories
abound, of course, some very ingenious. Did *nifty*
arise as a shortened form of *magnificat*? Is *gimmick*
from magicians' use of *gimac*, an anagram of *magic*?
But no word has attracted more theorising than *OK*.

Is it from Scottish *och aye*? Is it from French *au
quai* (the goods – or girls – have safely arrived 'at
the quayside')? Is it from Choctaw *oke* ('it is')? Is it
from Wolof *okeh* ('yes'). Is it from Latin *omnis korrecta*
('all correct', sometimes written by schoolmasters

15. *Residents of an estate in Fulham, London, celebrate the Queen's silver jubilee in 1977. Decades later, the slogan shows no sign of disappearing. When Kate Middleton married Prince William in 2011, the* Mail on Sunday *carried the headline: 'The Middle Class Rules OK.'*

on homework)? Is it from the Greek letters *omega* + *khi* (an early incantation against fleas)? Is it from *Obediah Kelly*, a railwayman who used to authorise freight movements with his initials? There are dozens more.

Thanks to a fine piece of research by American lexicographer Allan Walker Read, we now know that all of these theories are wrong. It first appeared in 1839 in a Boston newspaper, where there was a vogue for inventing humorous abbreviations using initial letters – an early instance of a language game. *KY*, for example, would be used for the phrase *know yuse* (= 'no use'). And *OK* comes from *oll korrect*, a humorous adaptation of the words *all correct*.

Why didn't it disappear, like the other abbreviations did? Because in 1840 it came to be associated with a totally different use – as a slogan during the 1840 US elections. It was the shortened form of *Old Kinderhook*, the nickname of President Martin Van Buren – Kinderhook being the name of his hometown in New York State. There was a *Democratic OK Club*, with its members called *the OKs*, and they had a war-cry: 'Down with the Whigs, boys, OK!'

The combination of the two usages, in a very short space of time, resulted in the rapid use of *OK* as an interjection meaning 'all right, good'. Other senses soon developed, such as 'fashionable' (*the OK thing to do*) and 'trustworthy' (*He's OK*). A century on, and the word was still developing new uses, such as 'comfortable' (*Are you OK with that?*). In British

English, it received huge graffiti exposure during the 1970s, when the fad of saying that someone or something *rules OK* (= 'is pre-eminent') was seen on walls all over the country.

But *OK* has a linguistic reputation for a second reason: the number of variant forms it has accumulated over the years. There are variant spellings (*okay, okey*), a shortened version (*'kay*) and several expanded forms (*okie-dokie, okey doke(s), okey-cokey*). Today, I suppose it's the basic *OK* form which is most often encountered, thanks to the dialogue button on our computer screens. Press *OK* and something will happen!

 ## *Ology*
suffix into word (19th century)

Suffixes, unlike prefixes (§87), are reluctant to become independent words, so when we find it happening, it's a notable moment. *Ology* is probably the most famous member of what is a very small club.

There have been *-ology* endings for a long time. *Theology* and *astrology* are two of the oldest, from the 14th century. More recent formations are *sociology* and *ecology*. Humorous and creative coinages abound, from James Joyce's *codology* ('hoaxing') to the *dragonology* of some children's books and the quirky titles of internet sites, such as *cheeseology*, *tattoo-ology* and (I kid you not) *fartology*. The ending means 'the science or discipline' of something, and comes from Greek *logos* ('word'). It literally translates as 'one who speaks in a certain way'.

Ology, as a noun for a science, is first recorded in 1811, and by the time Charles Dickens was writing it was in common use. In *Hard Times*, Mrs Gradgrind reflects to her daughter about her headmaster husband, 'a man of facts and calculations':

> You learnt a great deal, Louisa, and so did your brother. Ologies of all kinds from morning to night. If there is any Ology left, of any description, that has not been worn to rags in this house, all I can say is, I hope I shall never hear its name.

There certainly had been a flood of ologies in the previous century, many of them cheeky coinages such as *dogology* and *bugology*.

The usage is still with us. In the 1980s, actress Maureen Lipman, playing the part of Jewish matriarch Beattie in a series of British television commercials for British Telecom, is on the phone to her grandson, who has just admitted to failing most of his exams. However, he has passed sociology, to which she replies proudly: 'An ology! He gets an ology and he says he's failed! You get an ology, you're a scientist!' When the script-book was published in 1989, it was titled *You Got An Ology?* In 2000, this ad was voted 14th in Channel 4's 'The Hundred Greatest Adverts.

If an ology was a branch of knowledge, then an expert in that subject was an *ologist* – a usage first recorded in 1839. Anything related to an ology was *ological*. Mrs Gradgrind hopes Louisa will turn all her *ological studies* to good account. And anything related to an ologist would be *ologistic* – a usage which has been spotted just once, in the mid-19th century.

Few other suffixes have made such progress. People who have a strong like or dislike for something have sometimes been called *phils* or *philes* (for) and *phobes* (against). In medicine, a disease of a certain kind has sometimes been called an *itis*. They aren't common. The only ending that could compete with *ology* is *ism*. At least two reference books have been published with the title *Ologies and Isms*, listing all the subjects ending in these ways.

We first find *ism* as a separate word in the 16th century, usually in the plural, and in a context where the writer is being critical of religions (one writes: *Puritanism, Jesuitism, and other isms*). Dozens of coinages such as *Communism* and *Impressionism* led to *ism* being extended to movements in politics and art, and eventually to all kinds of beliefs and practices (a 20th-century writer: *isms like racism and sexism*). Today, the easiest way of being scornful about a set of topics is to call them *isms*.

During the 19th century, the word attracted its own endings. An adherent of an *ism* was an *ismatic*. Ismatics could be *ismatical*. The world of isms was *ismdom*. Turning a topic into an ism was to *ismatise* it. We only lack a record of *ismism*, and I'm sure this will turn up one day. In the meantime, the negative associations of the word are growing. There is now an internet site called the Institution of Silly and Meaningless Sayings: ISMS.

Y'all
a new pronoun (19th century)

The problem with saying *you* is that it's ambiguous – it can mean one addressee or several (§**69**). So it's hardly surprising that people have made up new forms to try to get round the problem. The obvious solution, following the usual pattern for nouns, is to make a new plural by simply 'adding an *s*', and this was one of the first variants to emerge. We find it recorded in Irish English in the early 19th century. *God bless yees!* says a character in one of Maria Edgeworth's tales. And the spellings began to proliferate: *yeez, yez, yiz*. The speaker was always talking to more than one person.

Similar forms developed elsewhere. *Yous* was another Irish creation, and it was probably this one which spread to various parts of England, Australia and the USA, often spelled *youse* and sometimes *yows*. But as it spread, it gradually lost its plural sense. Now just one person could be addressed as *yiz* or *youse*. I often heard it used like that, both as singular and plural, when I was a teenager in Liverpool. It was the same sort of development that had happened to *you* in the Middle Ages, once people stopped using *thou*. The ambiguity was back.

The *you* forms that developed in the USA showed a similar pattern of development. Dialect usages such as *yowe yens* from East Anglia probably travelled across in the *Mayflower*, and settled down as *youns* or *you-uns* in the eastern states. It's still used there today for both singular and plural addressees.

Y'all is the most famous of all the new pronouns. It's a shortened form of *you all*, first recorded in southern states of the USA in the early 19th century. Usage varies quite a bit, with some people restricting it to plural addressees and some using it for single addressees as well. It's the singular usage which can come as a shock to a British person, being addressed by *y'all* for the first time and realising that nobody else is included. When this first happened to me, in Texas in the 1960s, I was completely taken by surprise. As I entered a store, the assistant greeted me with a *Howdy, y'all*, and I actually looked round to see who else had come into the store with me. But there was only me there. And as I left he said *Y'all take care now*.

Nobody knows for certain whether *y'all* started out as a local usage among the southern black population or whether it was introduced by white immigrants. Either way, it rapidly established its presence, and then became more widely used throughout the country. It even travelled abroad, thanks to the many novels, movies and television serials reflecting life in the US south. *Y'all* is the usual spelling, but we'll also find *ya'll*, *yawl*, *yo-all* and others.

So, if *you* already exists in modern English, why use *y'all*? The two forms can be used for either singular or plural, so that can't be the reason. Is there a difference between saying *I hope to see y'all* and *I hope to see you*? Most people find *y'all* 'warmer' – a sign of familiarity, friendliness, informality or rapport. Some are still a bit suspicious of it and don't use it, perhaps because it reminds them of past ethnic tensions. But for many, today, it's simply customer-friendly.

Speech-craft
an Anglo-Saxonism (19th century)

It was only a matter of time before the huge influx of words from Latin, Greek and the Romance languages produced an antagonistic reaction. In the 16th century, the English scholar John Cheke thought English was being 'mangled' by all the classical words that were entering the language – the so-called 'ink-horn' terms (§41). And in the 20th century, George Orwell was a loud voice complaining about the way some writers went out of their way to use a Latin or Greek word when a good old Anglo-Saxon one would do.

Nobody took this position to such extremes as did the 19th-century Dorsetshire poet William Barnes. He felt that if all non-Germanic words could be removed from English, the language would immediately become much more accessible and intelligible.

So he looked for Anglo-Saxon replacements for foreign words. He resurrected long-dead words from Old English, such as *inwit* for *conscience* and *word-hoard* for *vocabulary*. And if there was no Old English word, he invented one. *Ornithology* became *birdlore*. *Pram* (*perambulator*) became *push-wainling*. *Alienate* became *unfrienden*. *Accelerate* became *onquicken*. *Arriving* and *departing* became *oncoming* and *offgoing*. The whole approach was described in his book *An Outline of English Speech-Craft*, published in 1878.

The interest continues today. In 1966, *Punch* celebrated the 900th anniversary of the Norman Conquest by having British humorist Paul Jennings translate passages of Shakespeare into what he called 'Anglish', such as Hamlet's famous soliloquy 'To be or not to be: that is the ask-thing'. And in 2009 David Cowley published *How We'd Talk if the English had Won in 1066*. He suggests hundreds of Anglo-Saxon equivalences; and several of his coinages, it has to be admitted, have a certain appeal, such as *sorrowword* for *lamentation*, *sameheart* for *unanimous* and *thankworthy* for *acceptable*. I think it unlikely that Alcoholics Anonymous will ever rechristen itself as *Unnamed Overdrinkers* or Americans start talking about the *Forthspell of Selfdom* (Declaration of Independence). But stranger things have happened, in the history of English.

DNA
scientific terminology (20th century)

It's much easier to have *DNA* as the heading for a chapter on scientific words than its full form: *deoxyribonucleic acid*. Far more people will recognise the first than the second. But both versions are typical of the way scientific language works. On the one hand, we find lengthy compound words; on the other, we find the abbreviations that make it possible for us to talk about these things without running out of breath.

Who knows how many scientific terms there are in English? One of the leading chemical dictionaries contains the names of around half a million compounds. How many species of insect are there? Well over a million have so far been identified. Plant species? Around 400,000. Presumably each of them has a name. There's little point in asking questions about totals when such large numbers are involved. No dictionary could ever hope to include them all (**§60**).

What general dictionaries do is include the terms from science and technology that are likely to have some currency outside of their specialised source. But even here the numbers are substantial. It's thought that around 80 per cent of the words in an unabridged English dictionary are going to be scientific terms. Where do they come from?

A large number come from Greek or Latin – anatomical terms, for example, such as *abdomen, femur, vertebra, cerebrum, trachea* and *thyroid*. But far more are the result of stringing together separate roots to make compound words of sometimes extraordinary length. *De-oxy-ribo-nucle-ic* is already quite complex at five elements. And that's the short version. In its full form it's actually cited as the longest scientific name by the *Guinness Book of Records*, with 16,569 elements.

Prefixes and suffixes are especially important. Scientific terms, of course, use everyday prefixes, such as *pre-*, *un-* and *de-*, but several have special scientific relevance. For example, great use is made of prefixes that express numbers (*bi-, mono-, poly-*) and metrical quantities (*nano-, micro-, pico-*). Some of these are becoming more familiar from their use in computing (§99). A few years ago, prefixes such as *kilo-, mega-* and *giga-* would have been obscure to most people, but today, thanks to *kilobytes, megabytes* and *gigabytes*, they are in everyday use.

The *-ic* of *nucleic* is one of several suffixes we associate with chemistry. Others include the *-ene* of *acetylene* and *benzene*, the *-ol* of *ethanol* and *alchohol*, the *-ium* of *chromium* and *sodium* and the *-ate* of *nitrate* and *sulphate*. But each science has its own distinctive forms, as suggested by botany's *spermatozoid*, geology's *cretaceous* and zoology's *stegosaurus*. Indeed, some of these suffixes are so distinctive that they can prompt errors in the unwary. In 2010 it was reported that a student, in an essay, thought a *thesaurus* was a species of dinosaur from *Jurassic Park*.

Garage
a pronunciation problem (20th century)

Words are identified through their spelling and their pronunciation, so it's a natural tendency to think that both are fixed. In fact, spelling often varies, as we have seen (§51). And we tend to underestimate the amount of variation that exists in pronunciation.

Choices vary between British and American English. Sometimes it's a straight swap: *tomahto* in Britain, *tomayto* in the US; the first syllable of *yoghurt* in Britain with the vowel of *dog* and in the US with the vowel of *oh*. Some US pronunciations have taken root in Britain: I normally say *schedule* with a *sh-*, but my children all say it with a *sk-*. As a result, I now use both pronunciations, and never quite know which one is going to pop up next in my speech.

In other cases, the situation is more complicated, because one of the dialects has alternatives. In British English, *vase* is 'vahz', whereas in American English some people say 'vaze' (rhyming with *haze*) and some 'vace' (rhyming with *place*). Conversely, in American English *glacier* is pronounced 'glaysher', whereas in British English it is either 'glassier' or 'glaysier'. *Garage* is like *glacier*. In America it is 'garahge', with the stress on the second syllable. In Britain it is either 'garahge' or 'garridge'.

Garage is a good word to choose as a reminder that pronunciation is always changing. When the BBC was formed, it set up an Advisory Committee on Spoken English to advise announcers how they should pronounce words which were unfamiliar or had competing usages. In their 1926 publication, they recommended 'garahge'. But by 1931 the members of the Committee had changed their mind. They say, '*Garage* has been granted unconditional British nationality, and may now be rhymed with *marriage* and *carriage*.' Both pronunciations are still heard today.

Several of the other BBC recommendations of the 1920s have long disappeared. They thought *fetish* should be pronounced 'feetish', and *Celtic* (the race, not the football team) as 'seltic'. They opted for *airplane*, not *aeroplane*. And they sometimes put the stress in places where hardly anybody – perhaps nobody – would put it now, such as *acumen*, *anchovy* and *precedence*. I have to say 'perhaps', because the old pronunciations could still be in the consciousness of some senior citizens, much as some continue to say 'forrid' for *forehead*.

Over half the words in a Pronouncing Dictionary will display alternative forms, though in many cases the differences are slight. Here are some of the more noticeable ones. Do you say the first letters of *either* with the sound of the vowel in *see* or in *sigh*? Do you say *example* with the *a* as in *cat* or as in *calm*? *Envelope* with the *e* of *hen* or the *o* of *on*? *Greasy* with the *s* of *see* or the *z* of *zoo*? Is it *a hotel* or *an 'otel* – or even *an hotel*? Does *tortoise* rhyme with *bus* or *voice*? Some stories depend on these variations, such as the one about the child who heard a priest ask the congregation to say 'the prayer that Jesus taught us' and wondered why Jesus had a pet. People who say *tortoice* don't seem to find it funny.

Escalator
word into name into word (20th century)

Imagine you invent something and you want to give it a name – say a device which automatically repairs non-functioning keys on computer keyboards. You think up a word which you think suits the product – *Keefiks*, shall we say, based on *key + fix* – check it hasn't been used by anyone else, protect it by registering a trademark and go into business. It takes off. You sell millions. And before you know it, the name has become part of the language. People talk about *keefiksing* their machines. The word becomes a metaphor. People start saying such things as *I'm keefiksing my apartment* and *I need a spiritual keefiks*.

You're quite pleased. And then along comes another firm with a keyboard-fixing technology that is different from yours, and people call it *the latest keefiks*, with a small *k*. You object. *Keefiks* should have a capital *K*, you insist. They'll have to call their product something else. You need to protect your brand. But it's too late. Other firms have already joined in. Shops start advertising *all keefiks models now in stock*. People ask for *a keefiks* for their birthday, regardless of make. A Hollywood movie about alien keyboard manipulators is called *Keefiks Attacks*. You appoint lawyers and go to court, arguing that others should not be using your word in this way. And you lose.

Dozens of real words have been through this scenario. One of the first was *escalator*. Various designs for moving staircase were invented in the 19th century, but the rights to the name *escalator* were purchased by the Otis Elevator Company. It was a word coined from *scala* (Latin, 'a ladder') with a prefix and suffix on analogy with *elevator*. It's first recorded in 1900, and within a few years it was being used figuratively. People talked of *escalator clauses* in contracts, referring to a planned increase in prices. Ambitious politicians were said to be on a *political escalator*. The verb *to escalate* appears in the 1920s, and *escalation* soon after. Otis tried hard to retain their control over the name, but in 1950 a court case concluded that the word had developed a general (or *generic*) meaning among the public, referring to any kind of 'moving stairway' and not just Otis's original design. Otis lost.

Several trademarks have become generic, over the years, such as *aspirin, butterscotch, heroin, thermos, yo-yo* and *zipper*. *Fedex, lego, meccano, kleenex, portakabin, rollerblade* and *hoover* have also become lower-case in some of their uses. A few companies have fought a battle to retain the rights over their name. Xerox Corporation, for example, has generally succeeded in persuading people to say *photocopy* instead of *xerox*. But most realise that they can't do much about controlling everyday usage. It's one of the penalties of success.

Internet names are the latest to attract generic use. The popularity of the Slashdot web site has generated a verb: *to be slashdotted* is to be overwhelmed with messages. Google has generated *to google*, meaning 'to search for information on the internet', regardless of which search engine is being used. Google has tried to prevent this extension in meaning, so far with some success. Several dictionaries now define the verb with reference to its originator, such as (in the *Oxford English Dictionary*) 'to use the Google search engine to find information on the Internet'. But whether this recognition has a long-term future, in the face of the steamroller of usage, remains to be seen.

Robot

a global journey (20th century)

In 1921, Karel Čapek's play *R.U.R.: Rossum's Universal Robots* had its premiere in Prague, and was translated into English for a New York production the following year. He needed a name for the factory-produced humanoid workers of the story, and was thinking of coining something based on the Latin word for 'work', *labor*. But his brother Josef suggested an old

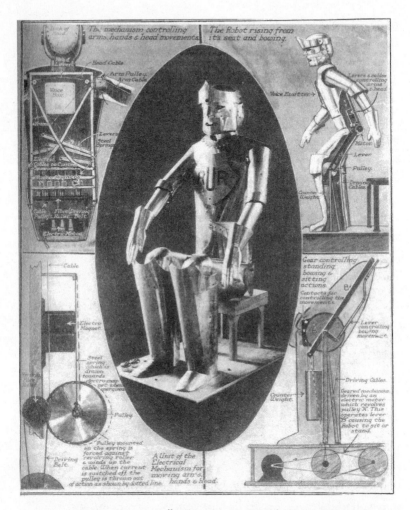

16. *A 1920 poster for Karel Čapek's play,* Rossum's Universal Robots. *Details in the poster show (top left) the mechanism controlling arms, hands and head movements, (top right) the robot rising from its seat and bowing, (bottom right) the gear controlling standing, bowing and sitting actions, and (bottom left) a unit of the electrical mechanism for moving hands, arms and head.*

Czech word for 'forced labour', *robota*. And *robot* was born.

If the Čapeks had known English, they might have opted for one of the words with relevant senses that were already in the language. *Automaton* had been available since the 17th century and *android* since the 18th. But the succinct punchy sound of *robot* seemed to capture the public imagination, because within five years it was being used not only for intelligent artificial beings but for any machine capable of carrying out a complex set of movements. An American newspaper in 1927 talked about different kinds of *electrical robots* that could answer the telephone, open doors and switch on lights.

Traffic robots arrived in 1929 – automated traffic lights. The earliest recorded usage is Canadian, but when I discussed the origins of *robot* in a BBC programme in 2010, several octogenarians from the north of England wrote to me to say they had clear memories of hearing the word used by their parents in this sense around that time. The London *Evening Standard* in August 1931 has the headline *Traffic 'Robots' in the City*. The northerners all pronounced it 'rowbow'. Nobody uses *robot* in that way in Britain any more, nor in the USA, Australia or New Zealand. But in South Africa the usage has stayed. People say such things as *Turn left at the robot* and *The robot's broken*.

The notion of a robot as an 'intelligent artificial being' continued to catch the public imagination. In real life, people talked about robot teachers, trains, petrol stations, planes and bombs. And in science fiction, the word took on new life, with writers such as Isaac Asimov writing acclaimed novels in which robots played a central role.

It was the science fiction writers who first shortened *robot* to *bot*, but none of them could have anticipated the explosion of usages which arrived in the 1990s, as the abbreviation came to be adopted in computing. Today, a *bot* is any piece of software that runs an automated task, such as in searching the internet or playing computer games. It has also become a suffix, with the function of the bot specified in the other part of the word, as in *searchbot, infobot, spambot, spybot* and *warbot*.

As early as 1923, George Bernard Shaw had applied the word *robot* to people who act mechanically, without emotion, usually because of the repetitive work they have to do. Now anyone accused of unthinking or automaton-like behaviour risks attracting the label. A movie star called Samantha who has taken on the same type of character too many times (in the eyes of the critic) might have her roles described as *Samanthabots*. And in 2009 *Obamabots* arrived – people who support Barack Obama without really knowing anything about him.

UFO

alternative forms (20th century)

Words can be shortened in several different ways, as other parts of this book illustrate (§§3, 57, 92). Abbreviations are a natural process. They save time and energy. They can save money, if the cost of a message depends on the number of letters it contains. And they can be a sign of social or professional identity. People who belong to the same group, such as doctors, lawyers and plumbers, tend to use the same abbreviations when they talk and write to each other.

It's an impossible task to list all the shortened words in a language, because new ones are always being created. The largest collections in English, such as Gale's *Acronyms, Initialisms and Abbreviations Dictionary*, contain well over half a million items. Note the title. This book is trying to ensure that all kinds of shortening are included – words like *info* ('information') and *poss* ('possible'), as well as *acronyms* (strings of letters pronounceable as words, such as *OPEC*, the 'Organization of the Petroleum Exporting Countries') and *initialisms* (where the individual letters are pronounced separately, such as *BBC*).

There are some interesting mixes of the two types. How do you say the word *UFO*? Is it 'you eff oh' or 'youfoh'? Both are possible. Similarly, some people pronounce internet *FAQs* as 'eff eh cues' and some as 'facks'. *LOL* in internet and texting slang means 'laughing out loud': it's pronounced either as 'ell oh ell' or as 'loll' (§94). In American English, a *VP* (vice-president) is sometimes a 'vee pee' and sometimes a 'veep' – and the spelling *veep* is quite often seen in print these days.

But what does *UFO* mean? For most people, it is 'unidentified flying object'. But for some it stands for 'Ultralight Flight Organisation'. In the British military, it could be a 'Unit Families Officer'. In physics it could be 'universal fibre optic'. In computing, 'user files online'. In medicine, an 'unidentified foreign object'. In the events that take place in online fantasy worlds, it stands for 'unwanted falling objects'. These are just some of the usages recorded in the dictionaries. There are at least twenty for *UFO*, and some acronyms have hundreds.

The 'flying saucer' sense of *UFO*, along with its 'youfoh' pronunciation, has allowed it to be the base for other words. In particular, the study of UFOs is called *ufology* and the students *ufologists*. *Ufological* and *ufoish* are also found. It's unusual for an acronym to generate a family of words in this way.

Acronyms are not just for technical and business uses. Many occur in everyday speech, and have done for centuries – *IOU* ('I owe you') dates from the 17th century, as do *NB*, *eg* and *pm*, all derived from Latin words, though most people would be unable to say what the letters stand for (*nota bene* 'note well', *exempli gratia* 'for the sake of example', *post meridiem* 'after noon'). *RIP* ('requiescat in pace', conveniently also 'rest in peace') and *RSVP* ('répondez s'il vous plaît') date from the 19th century. During the 20th century we find such forms as *ETA* ('estimated time of arrival'), *FYI* ('for your information') and *ASAP* ('as soon as possible'). The internet has also introduced a large number of acronyms, some motivated by the need to keep words as short as possible in text-messaging and tweeting (**§92**).

CD-ROM is an interesting mix, because it brings together an initialism (*CD*) and an acronym (*ROM*). The first part is sounded letter-by-letter, the second part is a whole word. Nobody would ever say 'see dee ahr oh em'. Similarly, *JPEG* files are pronounced 'jay peg'. Organisations which have three identical letters sometimes cheat: the American Automobile Association, or *AAA*, is often called *Triple A*. And *IOU* is unusual too, because it starts off as an acronym and ends up using a letter to replace a whole word. It should really be *IOY*.

Watergate
place-name into word (20th century)

On 17 June 1972 a group of men broke into the Democratic National Committee headquarters at the Watergate office complex in Washington. The evidence of Republican political involvement, and the attempted cover-up, grew into a national scandal which led to the resignation of President Nixon in 1974.

The political fallout was great, but the linguistic fallout was longer-lasting. The *-gate* suffix became a permanent feature of the language, used by the media to refer to any actual or alleged scandal or cover-up, political or otherwise – especially one which leads to the downfall of the implicated person. It was a very convenient form, short and to the point. Perfect for headlines (§88).

Most *-gate* words have a very short life, lasting only as long as a scandal remains news. Who now remembers what *Baftagate* was about in 1991? (A voting controversy surrounding the BAFTA film and television awards.) What was *Camillagate*? (A tape-recording of an intimate telephone conversation between the Prince of Wales and Camilla Parker-Bowles in 1992.) How long will *BP-gate* (from the 2010 oil-spill disaster) remain in the public domain? Or the repercussions of the Iraq War continue to be called *Iraq-gate*? Only one thing is certain: other coinages are waiting in the wings to replace them.

Place-names quite often end up as everyday words in English, developing a more general meaning in the process. People talk about *another Watergate*, meaning 'another scandal of the Watergate kind'. Governments and civil services become identified with their locations (*Whitehall, the White House*). Battles rarely make it into general use, with just a few exceptions, such as *balaclava* and *armageddon*. If you're engaged in a decisive and final contest of some kind, you will *meet your Waterloo*. And there is the remarkable verb use of *Trafalgar*, attested since the late 19th century in the phrase *Trafalgar Square* – to subject someone to a soap-box tirade. 'He just Trafalgar Squared me.' It's not common, but it's there in the dictionary records.

Most place-names enter the general language in relation to products. We readily make new nouns out of wine locations, and some become so widely used that they lose their capital letter. 'That's a lovely Bordeaux. Have a glass of champagne.' Other place-name drinks include *martini, cognac, port, sherry* and *bourbon*. The same applies to foodstuffs: *Brie* (cheese), *Brussels* (sprouts), *Danish* (pastries), *hamburgers, frankfurters* and *sardines* (from Sardinia). In the clothing world we find *jeans, jerseys, bikinis, tuxedos* and *duffle coats*.

But the process of making a word out of a place-name (a *toponym*) is widespread. Tell someone a limerick? Drive in a limousine? Own an alsatian or a labrador? Play badminton or rugby? Run in a marathon? Dance the mazurka? You never quite know where a place-name is going to turn up.

Doublespeak
weasel words (20th century)

In 1986, during the Australian 'spycatcher' trial, held to prevent the publication of a book by a former MI5 employee, the British cabinet secretary, Sir Robert Armstrong, was asked by one of the lawyers to explain the difference between a misleading impression and a lie. 'A lie is a straight untruth,' he said. The lawyer suggested that a misleading impression, then, was 'a sort of bent untruth'? Armstrong replied: 'As one person said, it is perhaps being "economical with the truth".'

He was referring to the 18th-century political philosopher Edmund Burke, who had once used the phrase 'economy of truth'. But that usage didn't enter the language in the way the new one did. To be *economical with the truth* came to be frequently quoted in the media and applied to other situations. It seems to have earned itself a permanent place in English idiom – one of the latest examples of *doublespeak*.

Doublespeak, or doubletalk, is a term known since the 1950s. It was prompted by George Orwell's novel *1984* – a blend of his *doublethink* and *newspeak*. It describes any words which deliberately hide or change a meaning in order to achieve an ulterior motive. As the chair of the US Committee on Public Doublespeak said in 1973, it is language

> which pretends to communicate, but really doesn't. It is language which tries to make the bad seem good, the negative seem positive, or the unpleasant seem attractive, or at least tolerable. It is language which avoids or shifts responsibility ...

The important point to stress is that this kind of language isn't the result of lazy thinking. Rather, it's the product of very clear thinking on someone's part. Doublespeak has been carefully selected in order to mislead.

A factory reports that they have had a leak of *biosolids* from their plant. They mean 'sewage'. An army reports a *surgical strike* on a town. They mean a 'military attack'. One company says it is *rightsizing*. It means people are being sacked. Another says it is offering *job flexibility*. It means there are no permanent contracts. There is the hint in these cases that the new situation is a good thing. *Bio-* suggests life. *Surgery* suggests cure. Words like *right* and *flexibility* put a positive spin on a bad situation. *Job seekers* sounds better than *unemployed*, *ethnic cleansing* better than *genocide*.

It all depends on your point of view, of course. If an army is on your side, it *intervenes* in another country; if it isn't, it *invades*. If an armed group is on your side, their members are *freedom fighters*; if not, they're *terrorists*. People can lapse into doublespeak for the best of intentions, believing they are really helping a cause. When a country is at war, few would doubt the importance of positive spin in maintaining national morale. When a company is worried about its share prices, it will do what it can to present itself in the best possible light.

But there comes a point when the public feels that the spin has gone too far, and several of the phrases highlighted by doublespeak campaigns – not only in the USA – have become so famous that they have lost their obscuring force. Everyone now knows what *friendly fire* means: you've killed your own men. And only the most hidebound of press officers would these days say *collateral damage* (for a raid in which bystanders are killed or injured) without embarrassment, because every journalist present would know exactly what was meant.

The Doublespeak Committee decided to give annual awards for the worst examples. In 2008 it gave the award to the phrase *aspirational goal* – as used, for instance, when talking about setting a deadline for withdrawing troops from Iraq or for reducing carbon emissions. The Committee observed:

> Aspirations and goals are the same thing; and yet when the terms are combined, the effect is to undermine them both, producing a phrase that means, in effect, 'a goal to which one does not aspire *all that much*'.

In other words: nobody has done anything about this yet.

How to reduce doublespeak? One way is to praise linguistic honesty; and the Committee does give Orwell Awards for good practice. Satire also helps. I especially like the report of a chess match in which one of the players proudly reports that he came second.

Doobry
useful nonsense (20th century)

Or *doobery, dooberry, doobrie, doobrey* … It's never obvious how to spell the invented forms we use to talk about an object whose name we don't know. Fortunately it isn't a problem, most of the time, because these nonsense words are usually used only when we speak. 'Where's the doobry?' someone might say, looking for the gadget which controls the television.

Doobry is the latest in a series of *doo-* forms that appeared during the 20th century. It's first recorded in British English in the 1970s. In earlier decades people used such forms as *doodah, doofer, doodad, doings* and *dooshanks*. *Doodah* seems to have been the first, recorded in 1928. *Doofer* came soon after, in the 1930s – probably derived from the phrase *do for*, as used in such sentences as *that'll do for now*. Workmen used to describe half a cigarette as a *doofer*. It became popular in Australia, where it also appeared as *doover* and *doovah*. In American English, the favoured forms, from early in the century, were *doohickey* and *doojigger*, and both are still used. *Doodad* also developed a more specific meaning in the USA, referring to fancy ornaments or articles of dress. There might be all kinds of doodads on a Xmas tree, for instance.

Nonsense words are a hugely useful feature of speech. They help us out when we're searching for a word and don't want to stop ourselves in mid-flow.

They're a lifeline in cases where we don't know what to call something, or have forgotten its name. And they're available when we feel that something is not worth a precise mention or we want to be deliberately vague. Their importance is illustrated by the remarkable number of these words that have been coined over the centuries.

The oldest ones, recorded in writing since the 16th century, and likely to be much older in speech, are based on the word *what*. In their full form they appear as *what do you call it/him/'em* ..., but they turn up in a wide range of contracted forms, such as *whatdicall'um, whatchicalt* and *whatd'ecalt*. Shakespeare uses one, when Touchstone addresses Jacques: 'Good even, good Mr what ye cal't' (*As You Like It*, III.iii.74). He's avoiding the pronunciation of the name *Jacques*, which would have sounded like 'jakes' in Elizabethan English – and *jakes* was a slang word for a toilet. Today the commonest forms are *whatchacallit* and *whatchamacallit* (from 'what-you-may-call-it').

The curious forms *giggombob, jiggembob* and *kickumbob* all appear in the early 17th century – usually in plays – but seem to have fallen out of use a century later. They were probably overtaken by forms based on *thing*. *Thingum* and *thingam* are both recorded in the 17th century, especially in American English, and there was a reduplicated form too: *thingum-thangum* (§56). Then, in the 18th century, when sensitivities about using unfashionable or inelegant words reached new heights, we find a raft of new creations: *thingy, thingummy, thingamerry, thingamajig, thingama-bob, thingummytite, thingumty, thingumtitoy.*

Nonsense words go in and out of fashion. Does anyone still use *jigamaree* or *whigmaleerie* nowadays? And what has happened to *oojah*? An issue of the *Washington Post* in July 1917 refers to new British army slang, and mentions *oojah* as coming from the East – from Arabic or Persian, perhaps. It was very common in forces slang during the Second World War, when it developed into such forms as *oojamaflop*. My Uncle Bill, ex-RAF, used that one all the time. But I don't think I've ever used it myself, except in articles like this one.

Blurb
a moment of arrival (20th century)

Is it ever possible to say exactly when a word was invented? Yes, if someone keeps a record (§**65, 66**). But more often we find new words known by the date the public got to know about them.

In 1906, the Huebsch company published a book by the American humorist Gelett Burgess, which sold very well. The next year, at a publishing trade association dinner, free copies were given out of a limited edition, printed – as was the association's custom – in a special dust jacket. Burgess had devised a jacket which showed a charming lady, Miss Belinda

YES, this is a "BLURB"!

All the Other Publishers commit them. Why Shouldn't We?

MISS
BELINDA
BLURB

IN
THE ACT OF
BLURBING

ARE YOU A BROMIDE?

BY

GELETT BURGESS

Say! Ain't this book a 90-H. P., six-cylinder Seller? If WE do say it as shouldn't, WE consider that this man Burgess has got Henry James locked into the coal-bin, telephoning for " Information "

WE expect to sell 350 copies of this great, grand book. It has gush and go to it, it has that Certain Something which makes you want to crawl through thirty miles of dense tropical jungle and bite somebody in the neck. No hero no heroine, nothing like that for OURS. but when you've *READ* this masterpiece, you'll know what a BOOK is, and you'll sic it onto your mother-in-law, your dentist and the pale youth who dips hot-air into Little Marjorie until 4 Q. M. in the front parlour. This book has 42-carat THRILLS in it. It fairly BURBLES. Ask the man at the counter what HE thinks of it! He's seen Janice Meredith faded to a mauve magenta. He's seen BLURBS before, and he's dead wise. He'll say:

This Book is the Proud Purple Penultimate ! !

17. The book jacket which introduced the word blurb into the English language in 1906.

Blurb, 'in the act of blurbing' – shouting out the title of the book and the name of its author. 'YES, this is a "BLURB"!' said the headline. The accompanying text was full of unbelievable praise: 'When you've *READ* this masterpiece, you'll know what a BOOK is'.

The word caught on. Any testimonial for a book, on front or back covers, was soon being called a *blurb*. In a little wordbook he wrote a few years later, Burgess defined his own term:

> A flamboyant advertisement; an inspired
> testimonial.
> Fulsome praise; a sound like a publisher.

And the word has been with us ever since. There is a blurb on the back of this book.

We don't know the exact moment that Burgess invented the word, but we do know that it began to circulate after that dinner. The same thing happened to the first artificial earth satellite, Sputnik 1, launched by the Russians on 4 October 1957. Before that, the word *sputnik* (translated as 'travelling companion') would have been known only to a small group in the Soviet Union. After the launch, it was everywhere.

The publication of a literary work has been the usual means of establishing the year in which a new word is introduced to the world. *Catch-22* arrived in 1961, following the publication of Joseph Heller's novel of that name. *Nymphet,* in the sense of a sexually attractive young girl, came in 1955 with Vladimir

Nabokov's *Lolita*. *Chortle* appeared first in Lewis Carroll's *Through the Looking-Glass* in 1871.

Cases of this kind are the closest we can get to the origins of a word. Usually all we can say is that the word appeared 'in the early 1960s' or 'in the late 14th century'. But the internet is changing everything (§49). If I activate the appropriate software, it is possible for the date, hour, minute and second at which I create a text to be time-stamped. And if that text happens to contain a new word, or a word in a new sense, its birthday will be known for ever.

Strine
a comic effect (20th century)

In 1964 the *Sydney Morning Herald* carried a story about what had happened to the English author Monica Dickens while she was signing copies of her latest book in a Sydney bookshop. A woman handed her a copy and said, 'Emma Chisit'. Dickens thought this was the woman's name, so she wrote 'To Emma Chisit' on the flyleaf. The would-be purchaser was puzzled. 'No. Emma Chisit', she repeated. Eventually it transpired that what she was saying was 'How much is it?' in an Australian accent. And Strine was born.

The story is told at the beginning of *Strine: The Complete Works of Professor Afferbeck Lauder* (real name: Alistair Morrison). *Strine* is the supposed Australian pronunciation of the word *Australian*. *Let Stalk Strine* was a best-seller when it appeared in 1965, and it's still in print. It contained such fine examples as *ebb tide* for 'appetite' (as in *I jess got no ebb tide these dyes*) and *cheque etcher* for 'did you get your' (as in *Where cheque etcher big blue wise?*). The idea caught on, and several compilations of supposed regional dialect speech were published in other parts of the world, such as *Lern Yerself Scouse* (for the dialect of Liverpool).

Words coined for comic effect don't usually become a permanent part of the language. If I start speaking in a mock way, putting on a dialect voice or pretending to use an old spelling-pronunciation (such as saying *yee oldee tea shoppee*), the effects are of the moment. Nobody would expect *oldee* to become a recognised pronunciation. But if a humorous form is used often enough, and begins to appear in novels and other literature, then it may well eventually enter the dictionary (with a warning that it is jocular). This is what has happened to *stoopid* (for *stupid*), recorded since Thackeray used it in *Vanity Fair* (1848), and *velly* (mock-Chinese 'very'), first recorded in the 1890s. Thanks to Rudyard Kipling and others, *squat-tez-vous* (mock-French for 'sit down') has achieved some usage. So has *el cheapo* (mock-Spanish for 'very cheap'), recorded since the 1950s. They're all in the *Oxford English Dictionary*.

Baby-talk can sometimes make its mark: *toothy-pegs, wakey-wakey, pussy-cat, beddy-byes, din-din, ickle*

18. The cover of the first 'strine' book, published in 1965.

('little'), *diddums* and *oopsie-daisy* are all examples of nursery language which adults use when they're being playful. Comic proper names can get into the language too. Dr Seuss introduced everyone to a *grinch* in *How the Grinch Stole Christmas* (1957), and the word is now quite common for a spoilsport or ill-tempered person. Cartoon characters can introduce or popularise a comic word, such as Homer Simpson's *D'oh*, Elmer Fudd's *wabbit*, the Flintstones' *Yabba dabba doo* and Mr Jinx's *I'll tear you meeces to pieces*.

Jocular forms of grammatically irregular verbs also sometimes achieve a widespread use. How often have you heard people say they're *fruz* or *froz*, instead of *frozen*? Or: Shakespeare *thought every thought that's ever been thunk*. Here too, literature can give these usages a blessing. Mark Twain is one of many whose characters *smole a smile*. James Joyce used *thunk* in *Finnegans Wake*. And so did Tigger in *Winnie-the-Pooh*.

Alzheimer's
surname into word (20th century)

Names are important in word-making. We've already seen how place-names can make words (**§80**) and first names (**§28**). Now it's the turn of surnames.

A remarkable variety of everyday objects come from the names of the people who invented them or who are closely associated with them. We find them in such areas as clothing (*cardigan, leotard, mackintosh*), including hats (*stetson*) and boots (*wellingtons*), food (*garibaldi, pavlova, sandwich*), flowers (*begonia, dahlia, magnolia*), musical instruments (*saxophone, sousaphone*) and guns (*colt, derringer, mauser*). Creative people, especially (if they're famous enough), can have their surname turn into a general word. Film buffs talk about a movie being *Hitchcockian*, and similar coinages are found in other areas of the arts, such as *Dickensian, Mozartian* and *Turnerian*. Language buffs who admire Henry Fowler's *Dictionary of Modern English Usage* have created no fewer than three adjectives to characterise his approach – *Fowlerian, Fowlerish* and *Fowleresque*.

Science, in particular, recognises achievements in this way. Think of all the names of physical constants that come from scientists, such as *ampere, celsius, hertz, ohm* and *watt*. Many terms in anatomy, physiology and medicine reflect their discoverers, such as the *Rolandic* and *Sylvian fissures* in the brain or the *Eustachian tube* between throat and ear. When diseases are person-named, they are usually shortened. So *Ménière's disease* becomes *Ménière's*, *Parkinson's disease* becomes *Parkinson's* and *Alzheimer's disease* becomes *Alzheimer's*.

Derived uses soon follow, as the case of Alzheimer's shows. The disease was first described by the German pathologist Alois Alzheimer in 1907, and the name was soon used as an adjective in such phrases as *Alzheimer patients* and *Alzheimer sufferers*, sometimes with an *'s* and sometimes not. By the 1930s, the name of the disease was being abbreviated to *Alzheimer's* or (especially in the USA) *Alzheimer*, even in medical journals. Concern over the effect of the disease grew in the early 2000s, so much so that it became one of the few diseases to be identified by an initial letter: *the big A*. (*The big C* – cancer – is another.)

Surnames that become common nouns and adjectives don't have to belong to a real person. English literature has provided several examples of characters who have given their name to a general situation. What would it mean to call someone *a Scrooge, a Cinderella, a Girl Friday, a Romeo*? In each case the situation described in the original book has been left behind, and the words are even sometimes written without the capital letters. Rather less usual is the use of two surnames together. *A Jekyll and Hyde personality. A David and Goliath situation. A Holmes and Watson relationship*. There aren't many of these.

Several fields go in for first name + surname. The world of roses, for example, has hundreds of examples of cultivars named after the whole name of an individual, including such well-known personalities as *Cary Grant* and *Bing Crosby*. And we'll find whole names in such domains as dog breeds (*Jack Russell*), ships (*USS Ronald Reagan*), locomotives (*Winston Churchill*), cocktails (*Rose Kennedy*) and cakes (*Sarah Bernhardt*). Titles are not ruled out (*Earl Grey* tea). These do lead to some unusual English sentences:

'Just smell that Cary Grant'; 'Would you like some Earl Grey?'; 'I'll have two Rose Kennedies.'

Grand
money slang (20th century)

Some areas of vocabulary are more productive than others. I once went through a dictionary pulling out all the ways there are in English for saying 'good' things about the world (such as *wonderful, happily, a marvel*) and all the ways there are for saying 'bad' things (such as *awful, clumsily, a disaster*). I found 1,772 expressions of positive sentiment and 3,158 expressions of negative sentiment. It's almost twice as easy to be critical in English, it seems.

Everyday concerns attract the largest vocabularies, especially as slang. Drugs, sex and booze have each generated hundreds of expressions. And so has money, both for the general meaning and for specific units and amounts. The different currency systems of English-speaking countries have added to the diversity (§31). Even old terms can live on in idioms: people still say in Britain that someone is *worth a few bob*, even though *bob* for a shilling ('12 old pence') disappeared decades ago. In Australian English we find *buckaroo* ('a dollar coin'), *brick* ('$10') and *shrapnel* ('small change'). In Jamaica, a *coil* is a 'roll of banknotes'. In Trinidad, a *dog* is a '$20 bill' – perhaps an echo of the days when people used *dog dollars* ('dollar coins where an original lion design had been worn away into something resembling a dog').

Slang words for 'money' vary greatly. Some go back hundreds of years. In Britain, *brass*, associated with the colour of gold coins, is found from the late 16th century. *Ready* (= 'ready money') is recorded from the 17th, now heard only in the plural *readies*. Also from the 17th century is *quid*, originally referring to a sovereign or guinea. It probably comes from the Latin word for 'what' (*quid*), which transmuted into a jocular sense of 'the wherewithal' at a time when Latin was widely known.

Cockney rhyming slang has given us several expressions. *Bread* is from *bread and honey* (= 'money'). *Five* ('£5') produces *beehive*; a *fiver* is a *lady* (from *Lady Godiva*). *Ten* ('£10') gives us *Big Ben* as well as *cock and hen*. *Eight* ('£8') is a *garden*, thanks to *garden gate*. Amounts and numerals sometimes appear as backslang: *dunop, evif, nevis, yennep*. The rhyming practice crossed the sea. In Australia we find *Oscar Asche* (an Australian actor of the early 20th century) for *cash*, *Oxford scholar* for *dollar* and *bugs bunny* for *money*. In South Africa, 'money' is sometimes called *tom* (from *tomfoolery* = 'jewellery'). And new rhyming slang is still being coined. In the late 20th century, we find *ayrton* as a word for '£10'. Why? Racing driver *Ayrton Senna* = *tenner*.

The USA has a huge range of slang expressions, some widely known thanks to their regular use in films and television, such as (for dollars) *bucks* and *greenbacks*, and (for money in general) *dough, potatoes, lettuce* and *cabbage* (the last two from the green colour of the banknotes). The origin of some of the words is a real puzzle. There has been plenty of speculation, but no firm conclusion, over *moolah* and *spondulicks* (both occurring in various spellings). And if I offer you *fifty smackers*, is this because people often kissed banknotes or plonked them down on the table? *Mazooma* is from Yiddish. So is *motza* (also in various spellings), used chiefly in Australia.

New words continue to arrive. The 20th century brought *lolly* (probably from *lollipop*) and *dosh* (perhaps related to a *doss*, 'a place to sleep in a common lodging-house'). A surprising development was *archer* for '£2,000'. It came from the court case involving British author Jeffrey Archer in which a bribe of this amount was alleged to have been used. It probably won't be part of the language for long.

The vast majority of these words stay in their country of origin. We don't find Americans describing dollars as quids or the British describing pounds as bucks. That's why *grand* is so interesting. It's one of the few money words to have travelled. First used in the USA in the early 1900s, meaning '$1,000', it was very quickly shortened to G. The term then transferred to British usage, meaning '£1,000'. British people happily talk about something costing *a grand*. But the digital age seems to have pushed G out of fashion. During the 1980s K, influenced chiefly by *kilobyte*, became the abbreviation of choice for 'thousand' in business plans and job advertisements. No city gent seems to earn *Gs* any more.

37 *Mega*
prefix into word (20th century)

Mega- became a popular prefix towards the end of the 19th century. Scientists found it a useful way of expressing something that was very large or abnormally large. So, a relatively large bacterium was called a *megabacterium*. As a unit of measurement, it expressed a millionfold increase, as in *megawatt*. And in the 20th century, from around the 1960s, it came to mean anything of great size or excellence. In the city, takeover bids involving large sums of money were *megabids*. Large shopping complexes were *megacentres*. An extremely successful song or film was a *megahit*. People attended *megafestivals*.

With all this *mega-* about, the stage was set for the prefix to become an independent word. And in the late 1960s, we find it being used to mean 'huge' (*Those are mega achievements*), 'excellent' (*That's a mega idea*) and 'very successful' (*She's mega in France*). It could even be a sentence on its own. A reaction to a brilliant stage performance might simply be an awed *Mega!*

Quite a few prefixes have started a life of their own as words. Garments and vehicles have been called *midis*, *minis* and *maxis*. If someone proposes a course of action, we can be *pro* or *anti* (or *con*). We can weigh up the *pros and cons*. If you're *an ex*, you're a former something – usually a former husband or wife, though any previous office-holder or member of an organisation could in principle be called one.

The words can go in various directions. If we hold extreme views, especially in politics or religion, we might be called *ultra*, or labelled one of the *ultras*. But *ultras* are also people who have extreme tastes in fashion. And since the 1970s a long-distance run of great length, especially one that is much greater than a marathon, has been called an *ultra*.

Multi- is another prefix that has developed a wide range of meanings as an independent word. If we heard the sentence *Multis are everywhere these days*, the speaker could be referring to cinemas (*multiplexes*), yachts (*multihulls*), buildings (designed for several families – *multi-family* houses), fashions (*multi-coloured*), very rich people (*multimillionaires*), bridge players (making an opening bid of two diamonds – *multi-purpose*), international businesses (*multinationals*) or products that contain a range of vitamins (*multivitamins*). This is really quite an exceptional range of senses, and all came to be used in the second half of the 20th century. *Multi*, in short, has become mega.

Gotcha

a non-standard spelling (20th century)

When *The Sun* reported the sinking of the Argentine cruiser *General Belgrano* in 1982, the headline attracted almost as much attention as the event itself: GOTCHA. And a generation on, it is the headline that has stayed in the popular mind. It was the non-standard spelling that caught the public imagination. The effect disappears when we re-spell it as GOT YOU.

Not everybody liked it. *Gotcha* has playful connotations. We say it when somebody is caught out in an argument or discovered in a game of hide-and-seek. Yet this was a story about war, with lives being lost. Many thought non-standard usage wasn't an appropriate choice for such an event. But few headlines have had such staying power.

A surprising number of words appear in non-standard spelling in newspaper headlines, novels, advertisements, graffiti and other written genres. *The Sun* has many famous instances, such as its claim after the 1992 election, IT'S THE SUN WOT WON IT. Often it's a pun that motivates the spelling, such as the headline reporting cases of swine flu in Britain: PIGS 'ERE.

There comes a point when a non-standard spelling becomes so frequently used that it gets into the dictionaries as an 'alternative' (**§61**). We'll find *gotcha* and *gotcher* in the *Oxford English Dictionary*,

THE Sun

QE2 IS SET TO SAIL FOR WAR

Liner may be turned back from a cruise

We told you first

NINE days ago The Sun said that the QE2 was to be called up. Everybody denied it. Yesterday the Ministry of Defence confirmed it. If you really want to know what's going on in the war buy The Sun. We try harder. See Page 2

GOTCHA

Our lads sink gunboat and hole cruiser

SUNK

AN Argie patrol boat like this one was sunk by missiles from Royal Navy helicopters after first opening fire on our lads

CRIPPLED THE Argie cruiser General Belgrano . . . put out of action by Tigerfish torpedoes from our super nuclear sub Conqueror

From TONY SNOW aboard HMS Invincible

THE NAVY had the Argies on their knees last night after a devastating double punch.

WALLOP: They torpedoed the 14,000-ton Argentina cruiser General Belgrano and left it a useless wreck.

WALLOP: Task Force helicopters sank one Argentine patrol boat and severely damaged another.

The Belgrano, which survived the Pearl Harbour attack when it belonged to the U.S. Navy, had been asking for trouble all day.

The cruiser, second largest in the Argy fleet, had been skirting the 200-mile war zone that Britain has set up around the Falkland Islands.

He believes the majority of crew members will decide not to sail in the South Atlantic.

So far I have heard from three seamen who want to go, the rest are non-committal or against joining the task force," Mr Cartwright said.

MAJOR

With its 15 six-inch guns our Navy high command were certain that it would have played a major part in any battle to retain the Falklands.

But the Belgrano and

BATTLE FOR THE ISLANDS

its 1,000 crew needn't worry about the war for some time now.

For the nuclear submarine Conqueror, captained by Commander Richard Wraith, let fly with two torpedoes.

The ship was not sunk and it is not clear there were many casualties there were.

HMS Conqueror was built at Cammell Laird's shipyard in Birkenhead for £2½million. She was launched in 1969 and

Continued on Page Two

UNION BOYCOTTS WAR

A UNION chief is blaming seamen on two ships Lives over by the Government. "Don't go to win the union can't protect you."

This astonishing advice comes from George Cartwright, the Communist leader at his National Union of Seamen's Felixstowe Port in Suffolk.

The Government has just requisitioned the Townsend Thoresen roll-on, roll-off vessels Baltic Ferry and Nordic Ferry.

'Folly'

The ferries will carry troops and battle equipment in support of the QE2.

Mr Cartwright told the 150 seamen: "Our advice is that it would be folly that if seamen put themselves under military command, they will no longer have our protection.

"I'm old enough to remember that one in three merchant seamen were killed in the last war.

"It is not a case of being unpatriotic. We are not at war and our advice is based on union practicalities.

"What we are saying is and gave our best advice.

Question

"There is no question of politics being behind the recommendation. We were asked for our view.

£50,000 BINGO! Today's lucky numbers are on Page 20

---

19. *The front page of* The Sun, *4 May 1982.*

first recorded in 1932, as well as *geddit?* ('get it?', 1976), *ya* ('you', 1941), *thanx* ('thanks', 1936), *gotta* ('got to', 1924) and *gonna* ('going to', 1913). In the 19th century we find *luv* ('love', 1898), *wanna* ('want to', 1896), *wiv* ('with', 1898), *dunno* ('don't know', 1842), *wot* ('what', 1829) and *cos* ('because', 1828). *Sorta* ('sort of') is recorded as early as 1790.

Have non-standard spellings ever become standard in recent times? The recorded examples suggest that their public presence is still quite limited. Because non-standard English is strongly associated with informal, jocular and intimate subject-matter, they typically occur in the creative, leisure, sports and comment pages of newspapers. *The Sun* is exceptional in using them for news. *Thru* for *through* has made great public progress in American English, where we also find it in compounds, such as *drive-thru, see-thru, sell-thru* and *click-thru*. But other forms seem to be restricted to special usages, such as Mr Chad's graffiti use of *Wot* (§10) or forms representing colloquial speech, such as *Sez who?*

Most often a non-standard spelling is an attempt to show a regional accent: *There's gold in tham thar hills, A man's gotta do what a man's gotta do, Gawd help us*. But we mustn't fall into the trap of thinking that only lower-class accents are the source of non-standard spelling. Upper-class speech can find its way into a non-standard spelling too: *huntin', shootin' and fishin'*; *dontcha know*; *she's a nice gel*.

89 PC

being politically correct (20th century)

Political correctness has been with us longer than its current vogue might lead us to think. The phrase *politically correct* turns up in the US Supreme Court as early as 1793, though not with reference to language. *Politically incorrect* is much more recent: the first recorded usage in the *Oxford English Dictionary* is 1933. And the abbreviation *PC* is the most recent of all: 1986. *PC* began its life with many positive associations. Today, when someone says that a word is *PC*, the connotations are almost always negative. What happened?

Political correctness is a linguistic movement which went out of control. Its supporters started out with the best of intentions, drawing attention to the way language can perpetuate undesirable social discrimination in such areas as race, gender, occupation and personal development. Feminists, for example, pointed to the way masculine words, idioms and word-endings reinforced a world-view in which women were ignored or played a secondary role (as seen in *all men are created equal, the man in the street, fireman, chairman*). The 'innocent' historical use of these expressions, they argued, was no guide. The goal had to be an inclusive language, which would avoid bias and give no offence.

In some cases, the solution was easy. It wasn't linguistically difficult to change *fireman* to *firefighter* or *all men* to *all people*. Other changes required more ingenuity (*air steward(ess)* to *flight attendant*), and in some cases (such as *man in the street*) the language provided no idiomatic equivalent at all. Some changes (such as *chairman* to *chairwoman, chairperson* or *chair*) proved controversial, on both sides of the gender divide, and some proposed replacements were disliked because of their awkwardness (such as using *he or she* for *he*). Many argued that the alternatives often did nothing to remove any prejudice there might be about the condition: what was the advantage of *persons with disabilities* over *the disabled*? The negative associations simply transferred to the new term, as seen with the search for a PC expression to describe people who are *handicapped/disabled/physically challenged/differently abled* ... or people who are *black/negro/coloured/Afro-American/African-American* ... And what was the point of changing a label if social conditions didn't change?

Problems grew when some PC activists took their linguistic case too far. Opposition to the word *black* in a racial context was one thing. Reading in racial prejudice behind all uses of the word *black* (as in *blackboards* and *black sheep*) was another. Stories circulated of authorities falling over backwards to avoid a word in case someone found it offensive. Some of the stories were true; some were myths reported by the media. It became difficult to distinguish truth from fiction. How many nursery school teachers heard the story that it was wrong to sing the nursery rhyme

'Baa baa black sheep', and that some other colour-word should be used instead? It probably started out as an urban myth (the 'rainbow sheep myth'), but I know teachers who have indeed changed the words, worried in case the parents of the one black child in their class might complain.

Fact or fiction, the political right focused on such stories as a means of discrediting the progressives who were trying to get a better deal for disadvantaged groups. Politicians always exaggerate the perceived weaknesses of the other side, and in the case of PC, numerous accusations were made about how excessive deference was being given to some groups at the expense of others. Insults flew. Those who drew attention to 'incorrect vocabulary' were charged with being 'thought police'. Moderate reformers found themselves grouped along with extremists.

Today, few people would describe themselves as being PC. Rather they admit, rather self-consciously but with a certain pride, to being 'non-PC'. They say such things as 'I know this is politically incorrect, but ...' and then they say what they have in mind. The PC movement has evidently had an effect, in that it has made them more conscious of the issues than they were before. But some disadvantaged groups might well be wondering what all the fuss has been about, for their situation hasn't changed a jot.

Bagonise
a nonce-word (20th century)

People love the opportunity to create new words. Newspapers and magazines hold competitions for 'words that should be in the language but aren't'. In the 1980s in the USA, comedian Rich Hall coined the term *sniglets* for his inventive lexical contributions to the show *Not Necessarily the News*. It was hugely popular; fans sent in their own ideas, and several collections were published.

I can personally confirm the popularity of the game, as I devoted one of the programmes in my BBC Radio 4 series *English Now* to it, and set listeners a competition. I got over a thousand proposals – far more entries than we received for any other competition. *Bagonise* was one of the winners. It means 'to anxiously wait for your suitcase to appear on the baggage claim carousel at an airport'. Another was *potspot*, 'that part of a toilet seat which causes the phone to ring the moment you sit on it'.

Sometimes the creativity lies in using old words in a new way. In the UK, Douglas Adams and John Lloyd published the best-selling *The Meaning of Liff* in 1983, in which place-names were given new meanings. *Goole*, for example, was 'the puddle on the bar into which the barman puts your change'. *Nantucket* was 'the secret pocket which eats your train ticket'.

These coinages are sometimes spontaneous, sometimes the result of a lot of thought; but they all have one thing in common. They are *nonce-words* – usages made up 'for the nonce'. The expression is from Middle English (*nonce* = 'once'), and in language study it refers to a word or phrase invented to meet the needs of a particular occasion. Nobody ever expects it to be used again.

Authors often invent a word in this way: there are hundreds in James Joyce, for example, such as *twingty to twangty too* (in *Finnegans Wake*: for 'twenty to twenty-two'). Lewis Carroll's coinages in 'Jabberwocky' (§67), such as *brillig* and *toves*, are noncewords. In the film *Mary Poppins*, there is the amazing *supercalifragilisticexpialidocious*. It's a feature of everyday conversation, too. In recent days I've heard someone say that a female bishop is a *bishopess* and a cake was *chocalicious*.

Sometimes a nonce-word catches on. When Joyce introduced *quark* into his novel, he could not have imagined that one day it would be adopted as the name of a subatomic particle in physics. And it only takes a famous person to use a nonce-word, consciously or unconsciously, and it can make headlines: in 2010, US politician Sarah Palin said *refudiate* – a blend of *refute* and *repudiate* – and was widely criticised for doing so. But, as she said in her defence, it's the sort of thing Shakespeare did. And indeed, if she – or George W. Bush – had said *compulsative* for *compulsory* or *irregulous* for *unruly*, they would have been condemned. But both are Shakespeare's.

Some people feel so strongly about the value

to the human race of their coinages that they use them as much as possible in the hope that one day they will get into the dictionary. The words that are most likely to have this happen are those which are invented several times independently. *Bag + agonise* is a fairly obvious combination, and as the circumstance is repeated millions of times every day it has probably been repeatedly coined. It's therefore only a matter of time before the word begins to appear in print. It already appears in the online Travel Industry Dictionary, labelled as 'slang'. That's a start. And in 2011 it had over 600 hits on Google. It's bound to become standard English one day.

Webzine
an internet compound (20th century)

In 1998, the American Dialect Society named *e-* the 'Word of the Year', the one 'most useful and most likely to succeed' (**§95**). It wasn't really a word, but they were right about its future. Thousands of e-coinages have since appeared, and many look set to be a permanent feature of the language, such as *e-books, e-conferences, e-voting, e-cards, e-money* and *e-zines*. *Web* was another success story, producing such phrases as *web design, web address, web page* and *web publishing*, as well as such compound words as *webcam, webcast, webmaster* and *webzine*. The proliferation began soon after the World Wide Web became public knowledge in 1991.

Webzine, for example, is recorded in 1994 – the latest in a line of other *-zines*, such as *e-zines*, *fanzines*, *cyberzines* and *amazines* ('amateur magazines'). You can find them in *zinestores* and celebrate them at *zine-fests*. If you are a regular reader, you are a *zinester*, and you may engage in *zineswapping*.

New compound words are one of the most notice-able features of internet vocabulary. Popular forms include *click* (*clickthrough rate*, *cost-per-click*, *double-click*), *net* (*netspeak*, *netiquette*, *netnews*), *ware* (*firm-ware*, *freeware*, *shareware*), *cyber* (*cyberspace*, *cyberculture*, *cybersex*) and *bot* (**§78**). Even the symbol @ has been made to do extra duty in word creation, both as a symbol and spelled out as a word (*@-address*, *atcom-mand*). Some very strange compounds have been created. If you look names up in a remote database, the usual instruction is *whois*. If you want to find a person's e-address by entering a name and location, you type in *whowhere*.

The internet has also favoured a previously rare phenomenon called *bicapitalisation* (the use of a capital in the middle as well as at the beginning of a word), notably in company names. We find *Alta-Vista*, not *Altavista* – and similarly, *AskJeeves*, *Com-puServe*, *DreamWorks* and *GeoCities*. Three capitals occur in *QuarkXPress* and *aRMadillo Online*. Some-times just a middle capital is used, as in the *i*-prefix usages which have produced *iMap*, *iPhone*, *iMac*, *iPad* and other innovations – a pattern which has been picked up and used in a wide range of contexts, such as *iDrugs*, *iDosing*, *iForms*, *i-Routes*, *iSense* and hundreds more.

Domain names are likely to turn the world of lexicography upside down. Virtually every word in everyday English has now been bought, to be used as a domain name. Familiar compounds have gone the same way. To invent a new domain name these days you have to be really ingenious and play with spelling or unusual sequences, such as *inventinganewword.com*. These are all proper names, of course, so they don't really count when it comes to vocabulary. But an unknown (and, I suspect, large) number will eventually develop general uses, in much the way that place-names have (§80). Do you wiki? Are you in a Mac-forum? Have you been Amazoned yet?

App
a killer abb (20th century)

In 1985 a writer in the trade newspaper *Information World*, describing a new kind of on-screen menu, used an abbreviation – and then felt he had better explain it: 'apps', he wrote, adding 'for applications'.

Most people would have needed an explanation at the time. The idea of an *application* – a computer function designed to meet a specific user requirement – had been around for over twenty years, but shortening it to *app* was a novelty. The word had never been abbreviated in that way before. It immediately caught on. There was something phonetically appealing about the short, perky syllable, which seemed to suit the exciting quickfire developments in digital communication of the time. And soon after, the idea of a *killer app* arrived – a function which, in the dreams of the multimedia industry, would be so appealing or superior that people wouldn't be able to do without it. If any word should achieve the status of a killer abb(reviation), it is this one.

There's nothing new about abbreviations, of course. They've been in English since its earliest days (§3). But the Anglo-Saxon scribes could hardly have predicted the extraordinary increase in shortened words and names that has taken place over the past century or so. One collection (§79) has over half a million abbreviations, with new editions adding thousands more each year. And no wordbook should ignore the way that electronic media generally, and the internet in particular, have become one of the most fruitful sources of present-day growth, especially in abbreviations consisting only of initial letters (*acronyms*) – *GPS* ('global positioning system'), *SMS* ('short messaging service'), *FAQs* ('frequently asked questions') and so on. Most are short – three letters is the norm. Just occasionally we encounter longer sequences, such as *WYSIWYG* ('what you see is what you get'), or some of the humorous strings found in text-messaging, such as ROTFLMAO ('rolling on the floor laughing my ass off').

How many of these will last? Many, especially those used in texting, are likely to have a short life (§94). But *app* seems a safe bet for a permanent place in the language. The number of apps are now in the hundreds of thousands, and mobile phones are increasingly the technology of choice for internet connection, so this is plainly an abbreviation that is not going to go away. Who would use four syllables (*applications*) in everyday speech when they can use one?

Cherry-picking
corporate speak (20th century)

This chapter is going to bring to the table a brain-dump of buzzworthy outcomes.

By close of play you'll have seen the value-added, the wow factor, of this joined-up state-of-the-art, blue-sky thinking. It'll be a no-brainer, a win-win situation, a foot-on-the-ball result. I'll be thinking out of the box. I'll cherry-pick the low-hanging fruit so that you'll see cutting-edge practice. Think synergy. Think mission. The bottom line is you'll take ownership of my visioning.

Cherry-pick, meaning 'choose selectively the most beneficial courses of action', is, like many other pieces of business jargon, a development of the 1960s. My pastiche is not unlike the 'corporate speak generators' that can be found online, producing strings of humorous nonsense – the humour, of course, lying in the fact that the results are uncomfortably close to the realities of what is daily heard and read in many offices.

What is going on? It isn't just a matter of jargon. Every profession, trade or social group has its special language – the technical terms, abbreviations and idioms which show that you are an electrician, lawyer, priest, journalist, doctor … To insiders, these terms are unproblematic: they define their professionalism. People only start condemning such language as jargon when the insiders talk to outsiders in an unthinking or pretentious way, using obscure words without considering the effect on their listeners.

Corporate speak is more than jargon. While such terms as *synergy, incentivise* and *leveraging* can be difficult to grasp, there's nothing especially hard about *wow factor, low-hanging fruit* or (at least to cricket fans) *close of play*. But these phrases nonetheless attract criticism. The charge is that, even though they are simple, they have lost their meaning through overuse. They have become automatic reactions, verbal tics, a replacement for intelligent thinking. In short, they have become inappropriately used clichés.

These days the charges come from both inside and outside the world of business management. And the criticisms are particularly harsh when other domains pick up corporate speak. Government departments especially have to be careful if they lapse into it. A UK parliamentary select committee in July 2009 examined the matter, and the chairman introduced the topic using another pastiche:

> Perhaps I could say, by way of introduction, welcome to our stakeholders. We look forward to our engagement, as we roll out our dialogue on a level playing field, so that, going forward in the public domain, we have a win-win step change that is fit for purpose across the piece.

Everyone in the room recognised the symptoms. And the subsequent discussion focused on the kinds of language routinely being used in government circles, such as *unlocking talent, partnership pathways, a quality and outcomes framework* and *best practice flowing readily to the frontline*. What could be done about it?

It's easier to identify symptoms than to suggest cures. And it's easy to parody. Eradicating habitual usage is hard. But there is a mood around these days that something has to be done. Whether in business or in government, recognising models of *good* practice, and rewarding them, will be an important first step.

LOL
textspeak (20th century)

When *LOL* first appeared on computer and mobile phone screens, it caused not a little confusion. Some people were using it to mean 'lots of love'. Others interpreted it as 'laughing out loud'. It was an ambiguity that couldn't last. Who knows how many budding relationships foundered in the early 2000s because recipients took the abbreviation the wrong way? Today it's settled down. Almost everyone now uses *LOL* in its 'laughing' sense. And it's one of the few text-messaging acronyms to have crossed the divide between writing and speech.

Dictionaries of text-messaging list hundreds of acronyms and give the impression that a new language, *textese*, has emerged. In fact, now that collections of real text messages have been made and studied, it transpires that only a few of those abbreviations are used with any frequency. Replacing *see* by *c, you* by *u* and *to* by *2* are some of the commonly used strategies. But the kind of message in which every word is an abbreviation (*thx 4 ur msg c u 18r*) is really rather unusual. On average, only about 10 per cent of the words in a text are abbreviated. And in many adult texting situations, textisms are frowned upon, or even banned, because the organisers know that not everyone will understand them.

The novelty of texting abbreviations has also been overestimated. Several were actually part of computer interaction in chatrooms long before texting arrived in the late 1990s. And some can be traced back over many years. In a poem called 'An Essay to Miss Catherine Jay', an anonymous author begins:

An S A now I mean 2 write
2 U sweet K T J ...

	West	East
Smile	:)	^.^
Sad	:(	-_-
Crying	:'(	;—;
Wink	;)	^_-
Shock/Surprise	:O	o_O
Grin/Big smile/LOL	:D	^O^
Angry	X-(	>_<
Kiss	:-X	^3^
Tongue out/Drooling	:p	°ㅜ°
Heart/Love	<3	*°.°

). *An illustration of cultural differences in the use of emoticons. In Western ountries, emoticons are viewed sideways and focus on the mouth; in the ast, they are horizontal and focus on the eyes.*

It was published in 1875. Lewis Carroll and Queen Victoria are among the many Victorians who played with such sound/letter substitutions.

On the other hand, there's nothing in older usage that quite lives up to the modern penchant for taking an abbreviation and adding to it. Thus, from the basic form *imo* ('in my opinion') we find *imho* ('in my humble opinion'), *imhbco* ('in my humble but correct opinion') and *imnsho* ('in my not so humble opinion'). And a similar thing happens to the other big innovation of contemporary electronic communication: the emoticon or smiley. Based on :), used to express a friendly reaction, we find :)), :))) and other extensions conveying increased intensity of warmth.

It's difficult to say how many of the novel computer abbreviations will remain in the language, once the novelty has worn off. *Txt, txtng* and related forms may survive, but only as long as the technology does. And who can say whether, in fifty years' time, people will still be typing such forms as *brb* ('be right back') and *afaik* ('as far as I know') and sending each other combinations of cat pictures + non-standard grammar (*lolcats*)? Will there still be keyboards and keypads then, even, or will everything be done through automatic speech recognition? With electronic communication, as I said earlier (§32), we ain't seen nothin' yet.

Jazz
word of the century (20th century)

Since 1990, members of the American Dialect Society have voted on the 'Word of the Year' (**§91**). The selection reflects social as much as linguistic factors. In 1999, they chose *Y2K*. In 2001, *9–11*. And the economic crisis of recent years is reflected in *subprime* for their 2007 choice and *bailout* for 2008. It's thus something of a relief to find *tweet* their selection for 2009 (**§100**).

Choosing a word for a year is difficult enough. Much more difficult is a 'Word of the Decade'. In 2010 the members of the Society chose *google*. That seems fair enough. But what would you do for the 'Word of the Century'?

They chose *jazz*. It was perhaps bending the truth a little, but not much. The word doesn't surface until the century is over ten years old. In 1913, a San Francisco commentator described *jazz* as 'a futurist word which has just joined the language'. However, he wasn't referring to the musical sense, which didn't arrive until a couple of years later. He meant *jazz* as a slang term for 'pep' or 'excitement'. It also meant 'excessive talk, nonsense'. This general sense is still known in the expression *and all that jazz*, meaning 'and stuff like that'. As an adjective, it developed a wide range of senses – 'lively', 'vivid', 'sophisticated'. There were *jazz dances* and *jazz patterns* (in clothing and furniture); there was *jazz journalism* and *jazz language*. Today we'd say *jazzy*.

The music sense is first recorded in the Chicago press of 1915 – and it quickly took off. It was used to describe hundreds of notions associated with the music – types of music (*jazz blues, jazz classics*), musical instruments (*jazz guitar, jazz clarinet*), players and singers (*jazz pianist, jazz vocalist*) and performing groups (*jazz quartet, jazz combo*). Virtually all the terms we now associate with jazz (*band, club, music, singer, records*) were in use by the end of the 1920s.

The word acquired more applications as the century progressed. New musical trends motivate fusions, so we find such phrases as *jazz-rock, jazz-funk* and *jazz-rap*. In the 1950s and '60s, we encounter *jazzetry* ('reading poetry to jazz') and *jazzercise* ('performing physical exercises to jazz'). In the 1990s, we find *jazz cigarettes* ('marijuana').

The early practitioners of jazz knew that they were living through a musical revolution: *jazz era* is first used in 1919; *jazz age* in 1920. Not everyone would agree with the voting of the Society members, which probably reflects their musical interests as much as anything else, but to my mind it was quite a good choice.

Sudoku
a modern loan (21st century)

Sudoku has been in Japanese at least since the 1980s, when the game was first devised, but it didn't appear as a loanword in English until 2000, one of the first borrowings of the new millennium. It continued a trend to take words from Japanese that had been building up in the second half of the 20th century.

Karaoke seems to have been with us for ever, but its first recorded use in English is only 1979. And since 1950 increased tourism and international business has brought hundreds of words into English from Japanese, many quite specialised. If you're into *sumo* wrestling, for example, your loanwords will be quite extensive, such as *yokozuna* ('highest rank of wrestler'), *dohyo* ('the sumo ring'), *okuridashi* ('a pushing technique') and *torikumi* ('a bout'). The business world will make you familiar with *shoshas* ('trading houses'), *kanban* ('a just-in-time production method'), *kaizen* ('improvements in practice') and *zaitech* ('financial engineering').

Gardeners will know *bonsai* ('dwarf plants'). Film buffs will know *anime* ('animated films'). Artists will know *shunga* ('erotic art'). Those who practise alternative medicine will know *shiatsu* ('a finger-pressure therapy'). Martial arts practitioners will know *shuriken* ('a type of weapon') and, of course, *karate*. Cooks will know *dashi* ('cooking stock'), *tamari* ('soy sauce') and *teriyaki* ('a type of fish or meat dish').

Tourists will have travelled on the *Shinkansen* train and perhaps stayed in a *ryokan* ('a traditional inn'). Hopefully they will not have encountered a *yakuza* ('gangster'). At home they may still have a rusting *Betamax* – a name often thought to be a Greek coinage, but in fact from Japanese *beta* 'all over' + *max(imum)*.

However, the trend seems to be slowing down. Very few 21st-century new words in English have so far been borrowings. *Vuvuzela* is a South African example from 2010, but it took an event of World Cup proportions to introduce it. Does this reflect a new national concern over identity?

 ## 97 *Muggle*
a fiction word (21st century)

Much of the new vocabulary in 21st-century English reflects the major social changes and events that have taken place in the real world. New editions of dictionaries in the 2000s have included such expressions as *social media, congestion charge, designer baby, flash mob, toxic debt, quantitative easing, geoengineering, WMDs* ('weapons of mass destruction') and *wardrobe malfunction*. More interesting, because more unexpected, are the words that have come from the world of fiction.

J. K. Rowling coined *muggle* in her first *Harry Potter* novel (1997) for a person who possesses no magical powers – adapting the associations of *mug* in the sense of 'foolish or incompetent person' and somehow neatly bypassing its earlier senses. Nobody would have linked it to the 13th-century use of *muggle* meaning 'fish-like tail' or the 17th-century use meaning 'sweetheart', but I'm surprised it survived the sense of 'marijuana' in American street slang, which had been around for most of the 20th century. Marijuana addicts were *mugglers*. It didn't seem to matter, as the power of the *Harry Potter* series grew.

By the turn of the millennium, the word had travelled well beyond the books and films. A *muggle* in the 2000s is any person thought to lack a particular skill. Some people use it in the same way as its source word, *mug*, and there are similarities too with the way *muppet* (a term popularised in the 1970s by Jim Henson) has left puppetry behind to mean – usually as an affectionate tease – an 'idiotic or inept person'.

An unexpected development arose in the high-tech treasure-hunting game known as *geocaching*, devised in 2000, where people who don't know the game or who interfere with it in some way are described as *muggles*. Adventurers equipped with a GPS system try to locate hidden containers (*geocaches*) around the world, using geographic co-ordinates registered on the geocaching web site. If a geocache has been vandalised or stolen, it's said to have been *muggled*.

Films have introduced hundreds of catch-phrases into English, such as *Make my day!* and *May the Force be with you*. Only occasionally, as we saw with *matrix* (§37), have they also provided new words, or new senses of old words. *Muggle* is one of those cases. And since 2000 we should also give due recognition to *Winnie-the-Pooh*, which has popularised *tiggerish* ('very lively, cheerily energetic'), *Austin Powers*, which has introduced us to *mini-me* ('a person closely resembling a smaller version of another') and *Meet the Fockers*, for *fockerise* ('to introduce comedic chaos of the kind displayed in the film').

Television advertising has also been a rich source of catch-phrases and the occasional new word or sense, though these rarely travel outside the countries where an ad is shown. *Pinta* ('pint of milk') entered British English in the late 1950s because of its use in the television jingle *Drinka pinta milka day*. And in the 2000s we find *va-va-voom*, used as an expression of admiration since the 1950s, but not widely known until it became the theme of a series of UK television commercials for Renault cars, starring footballer Thierry Henry, in which he tried to track down its real meaning. 'Look,' he says apologetically in one of the ads, 'I don't make the words.' But without him, I doubt if we would now have its latest meaning: 'the quality of being exciting, vigorous or attractive'.

Chillax
a fashionable blend (21st century)

This combination of *chill* (in its 'calm down' sense) and *relax* arrived in the early 2000s – a coinage which has come to be loved and hated in about equal proportions. By 2010 it had become a newsworthy headline. A piece by Simon Hoggart in *The Independent* for 23rd February began: '*Chillax man – or Gordon will get you*' – apparently referring to the then prime minister's use of the word while telling his advisers not to panic. If Gordon had been really cool, of course, he would have used the derived expression: *Chillax to the max*.

This is one of the latest blends, or portmanteau words – a technique of word creation (**§67**) that has become extremely popular in the 21st century. *Chillax* is gradually building up a word family of its own: already we have *chillaxing* and *chillaxed*. *Podcast* – a blend of *iPod* and *broadcast* – is even more productive: first used in 2004, it's now found as a noun (*a podcast*), a verb (*to podcast*), an adjective (*a podcast experience*) and in several derived forms (*podcasting, podcasters, a podcasted show*).

Dozens of new blends are around now: have you seen a *threequel* (a 'second sequel'), eaten *turducken* ('a combination of roast chicken, duck and turkey'), read about a *bromance* ('affection between two men'), taken a *staycation* ('vacation staying at home, or in one's home country') or *daycation* ('a day-long holiday') or used a *freemium* ('an internet business model in which basic features are free but advanced features are not')? You may have *frenemies* ('people with whom you remain friendly, despite some sort of dislike'). You will certainly know some *screenagers* ('teens who have an aptitude for computers and the internet').

And what about *jeggings*? These are leggings designed to look like tight-fitting jeans, a blend of *jeans + leggings*, and one of the most fashionable clothing developments of 2010. The word family here is growing: *meggings* ('men + leggings'), *treggings* ('trousers + leggings'). It seems to be a trend within the fashion industry to mix different types of clothing, and the language is desperately trying to keep up. Have you worn a *coatigan* ('coat + cardigan'), *shacket* ('shirt + jacket'), *skorts* ('skirt + shorts') or *tankini* ('tank top + bikini')? Or a *mankini* ('man + bikini', male skimpy swimwear such as that used by the film character Borat)? Then there are *blurts* ('blouse + skirt'), *cardigowns* ('cardigan + dressing gown'), *mackets* ('mac + jacket'), *shoots* ('shoe + boot') and *skousers* ('skirt + trousers'). I sometimes wonder which came first – the design or the word?

99 *Unfriend*
a new age (21st century)

In 2009 the *New Oxford American Dictionary* chose *unfriend* as its 'Word of the Year'. It meant 'to remove someone from a list of contacts on a social networking site such as Facebook'. A minor controversy followed. Some argued that the verb should be *defriend*. But the use of *un-* was already well established in the terminology of reversing computer actions, with *undo, unerase, undelete, unbold* and many more. As a *New York Times* article said in 2009 (15th September), we are living in an 'Age of Undoing'.

Unfriend also probably appealed because it feels more English, as evidenced by a history of earlier uses dating from the 16th century (§44). Antonio describes Sebastian as 'unguided and unfriended' in *Twelfth Night* (III.iii.10). A noun (*an unfriend*) occurs as early as the 13th century. And in the 19th century, a member of the Society of Friends (the Quakers) could describe a non-member as an *unfriend*. *Defriend*, by contrast, had no such history, so it has been slower to take root. But both *unfriend* and *defriend* are found in the social networking world now, with *unfriend* almost twice as popular in 2011.

Prefixes and suffixes continue to make their presence felt in word coinages of the new millennium. We find *ecogloom* ('depression about environmental progress') and *bargainous* ('relatively cheap'), *overthink* ('think about something too much') and *underbudget* ('underestimate costs'), *catastrophise* ('present a situation as worse than it is') and *therapise* ('provide therapy'). As technology allows us to investigate smaller and smaller entities, previously obscure prefixes such as *nano-* have become widespread. It is, according to some commentators, a *nano-age*, with a *nanocosm* containing *nanomachines* using *nanomaterials* on a *nanoscale*, and investigated by *nanoscientists*. Virtually any word, it seems, is going to be prefixed by *nano-* sooner or later.

Nano- has left *micro-* a long way behind, though *micro-* did receive a boost with the advent of *micromessaging*. The posting of very short entries on a blog came to be called *microblogging*, and when Twitter arrived in 2006, with its 140-character message limitation, it was soon being described as a *microblogging site*. There are *microbooks, micromovies, micromusicals* and (§92) *microapps* now. Speaking as a lexical coolhunter (a 1990s' marketing term: 'a monitor of cultural trends'), I wouldn't write it off yet.

Twittersphere
future directions? (21st century)

It's remarkable how a single sound can be taken to heart and used as a source of fresh word formation. In 2010, around 600 new words were listed in *Twittonary*, one of the online dictionaries collecting terms invented in connection with Twitter. That's an amazing total, given that this web site had then been in existence for only five years.

Most of the words are the result of people exploiting the playful possibilities in the name, especially those suggested by the unusual (in English) phonetic properties of the initial consonant cluster *tw-*. Two-thirds of the entries play with that cluster. Some replace an initial consonant, as in *twictionary* and *tweologism*. Some pretend to be a speech defect, replacing a *tr-* word, as in *twendy* and *twaffic*. Some add the cluster to the beginning of another word, as in *twidentity theft* and *twaddiction*. Blends are also very common, as in *twitterhea, twitterati, twitterholic, celebritweet* – and, summarising its entire world, *twittersphere*.

Most of these creations are likely to have a short linguistic life. Just a few will be long-term additions to the language – or, at least, for as long as Twitter exists. We can see this from what happened to an earlier internet phenomenon – blogging. In the early 2000s, the word *blog* (an abbreviation of *web log*, an individual's online diary or commentary) also generated a great deal of wordplay, but some of the coinages that were popular then are hardly ever seen these days.

The same word-building processes are found in the *blogosphere* as we find in the *twittersphere*. There's the same sort of substitution of clusters (*blargon*, 'blog jargon') and syllables (*blogathy*, 'blog apathy') and a similar range of blends (*blogorrhea, blogerati,*

blogoholic, celebriblog). The unique phonetic properties of the core term are also exploited: internal
rhyme is seen in *bloggerel, lexiblography* and *blogsti-
pation* (the sad state of affairs when a blogger can't
think of anything to say).

Rather more technical are such blends as *blog-
roll* and *blogware, photoblog* and *moblog* ('posts sent
by mobile phone'), or *blawg* ('law blog') and *vlog*
('video blog'), and such compounds as *blog client*
and *blog archive*. These are the terms which seem to
have achieved a long-term place in the language –
though again, this will be the case for only as long
as the technology exists. Important too are well-
established words which have been given a new
sense in the context of blogging, such as *gadget, post,
preview, archive* and *template*.

As for Twitter, if you had asked me as recently as
2005 whether I thought there was anything interesting about the consonant cluster *tw*, I would have
said 'nothing at all'. If you had suggested that one
day it would be the basis for coining hundreds of
new words, I would have said you were mad. Moral:
word buffs should never try to predict the future.

Illustration credits

Word index